notice.

Wedding and Pic-Nic Parties attended with Four Horse Omnibuses, if required.

Good accommodation for Hunters in the season. Horses taken in to Livery and Bait.

ELIZABETH BICKERTON,

"SWAN"

COMMERCIAL HOTEL,

WILMSLOW.

Commercial Gentlemen and Visitors to Wilmslow and the neighbourhood will meet with every comfort and ac[illegible]- modation at the above Hotel.

WINES AND SPIRITS OF THE CHOICEST QUAL[illegible].

PRIVATE FAMILIES SUPPLIED.

BASS'S PALE AND OTHER BURTON AL[illegible].

☞ A Large Room, suitable for Public Meetings, Agricultural Dinn[illegible] and other purposes.

The Old Community

A Portrait of Wilmslow

for the growing good of the world is partly
dependent on unhistoric acts; and that things
are not so ill with you and me as they might
have been is half owing to the number who
lived faithfully a hidden life, and rest in
unvisited tombs

GEORGE ELIOT, *Middlemarch.*

The Old Community

A Portrait of Wilmslow

By Howard Hodson

The Hampsfell Press
18 Manor Close, Wilmslow
1974

I.S.B.N. 0 9502103 1 5

Made and printed in Great Britain by
The William Morris Press Ltd
Wythenshawe, Manchester

DESIGN BY MICHAEL CANE

Introduction

This book attempts to evoke the spirit of a place through its pictures, its documents, its landscape, its recollections. It has been said that Wilmslow has no history, but the history of any place is at least the sum of the lives of all its inhabitants. There is a story told by Evelyn Waugh of standing one evening on the terrace of Sir George Sitwell's mansion at Renishaw in Derbyshire: 'In the valley at our feet . . . lay farms, cottages, villas, the railway, the colliery and the densely teeming streets of the men who worked there . . . [Sir George] turned and spoke in the wistful, nostalgic tones of a castaway, yet of a castaway who was reconciled to his solitude. "You see", he said, "there is *no one* between us and the Locker-Lampsons" '. In similar vein the admirable Earwaker, devoting one page of his monumental *East Cheshire* to the industrial village of Bollington, explains that, as the place has no manor or manorial rights, but simply lands held by smallholders, 'there is therefore no history to narrate'. To neighbouring Pott Shrigley he gives eighteen pages, half of them occupied by genealogies of the Downes, the Shrigleys, and the Potts.

Today we take greater cognizance of more ordinary folk—the 'small change' dismissed by Napoleon as he surveyed the dead after the battle of Eylau. One is poignantly aware of the undiscovered richness of unchronicled lives when leafing through the enormous burial register of some great nineteenth century city cemetery, or when standing in a once tiny churchyard like Wilmslow's which between 1558 and 1829 received 10,700 recorded burials. Even the aristocratic eighteenth century could occasionally sense the richness of poor lives. Gray's lines on 'the rude Forefathers of the hamlet', 'each in his narrow cell for ever laid' are so well-worn as to seem now sentimental; but listened to afresh they convey sharply the feeling of ordinary lives actually lived: the physical and emotional warmth of home, the central role of the mother, the organic relationship between man and his work:

> For them no more the blazing hearth shall burn,
> Or busy housewife ply her evening care:
> No children run to lisp their sire's return,
> Or climb his knees the envied kiss to share.

> Oft did the harvest to their sickle yield,
> Their furrow oft the stubborn glebe has broke:
> How jocund did they drive their team afield!
> How bow'd the woods beneath their sturdy stroke!

We are all aware of the inward richness of our own and our family's lives. Yet this richness—ultimately of significance surpassing the impact of any external events—is quite outside the ambit of traditional history. Maybe it is better revealed in the novelist's sensitive recreation:

> Paul saw drops of sweat fall from his father's brow. Six men were in the room—six coatless men, with yielding, struggling limbs, filling the room and knocking against the furniture. The coffin veered, and was gently lowered on to the chairs. The sweat fell from Morel's face on its boards.
>
> 'My word, he's a weight!' said a man, and the five miners sighed, bowed, and, trembling with the struggle, descended the steps again, closing the door behind them.
>
> The family was alone in the parlour with the great polished box. William, when laid out, was six feet four inches long. Like a monument lay the bright brown, ponderous coffin. Paul thought it would never be got out of the room again. His mother was stroking the polished wood.

This feeling of the significance of ordinary lives is very present also in Hardy; perhaps it is no accident that the title of one of his novels is taken from Gray's *Elegy*. Most of Hardy's stories are about a way of life which he had known but which was passing away in his life time. A historian of English local life like W.G. Hoskins (who himself has said we know little about the history of the English family) sees it as his task to recreate this society which existed from time immemorial but which the nineteenth century largely destroyed; he calls it 'the old community', and to describe it he quotes from Eric Gill:

> Up to the nineteenth century . . . men had depended on their own exertions to win a living from the earth . . . This world, a world dependent upon human muscular power, the muscular power of draught animals, was a product of many thousands of years of development. It was not a primitive world, it was not an uncivilised world, above all it was not an uncultured world. All the primary needs of humanity, material and spiritual, were met and met adequately . . . it was a hand-made world throughout, a slow world, a world without power, a world in which all things were made one by one.

How much better than this life of the past is life today? Andrew Pearson, celebrating Queen Victoria's 'long reign and diamond jubilee' in his *Wilmslow: past and present*, had no doubts:

> Sometimes we do hear men talk strangely of the good old times, and occasionally hear them express a wish that they had been born in the world's past; but surely, such is only the romance of bygone days. It is all very well to think how nice it would have been to be a knight in the past, dressed in a metal pot hat, a sheet iron overcoat, a pair of cast iron breeches, long spear in hand, and a horse dressed up to match . . . but when you think of having to sleep on a mud floor, in a room without stove or warm clothing, surely the romance of the past dies . . . there never was a better time to live than in the present. We have luxuries in plenty to-day, which in the past could not be had for love or money . . . it may be truly said we are living in the sunny days of England.

No doubt this is very true; and even, perhaps, more so today than in 1897 (twelve years after Pearson wrote, Stephen Beswick was taken to Bucklow Union Workhouse having spent two and a half years living in a bacon box at the top of Manchester Road). What still remains uncertain is the emotional quality of ordinary people's lives in the past. Hoskins has calculated that in the early sixteenth century two-thirds of the population of the larger English towns were living below or very near the poverty line. Professor Everitt reckons that in the sixteenth and early seventeenth centuries labourers formed between a quarter and a third of the rural population, and that by the end of the seventeenth century, with cottagers and paupers, they comprised nearly a half of the population of the whole country. If this great slice of English people suffered physically, how did they fare emotionally? In contrast to our socially fragmented existence of today we would like to detect a more coherent, meaningful, integrated life in the past. Such qualities have been seen, for instance by Eric Gill and F.R. Leavis, in the life and work of pre-industrial craftsmen; but craftsmen must have been a small proportion of Hoskins' and Everitt's urban and rural poor, and have become smaller. However, Everitt suggests that farmwork itself was not all 'unrelieved hardship and monotony'. In a sample of about three hundred labourers' probate inventories between 1500 and 1640 he finds mention of sixty different kinds of tools and farm-gear; and a well furnished labourer, whose whole wealth at death did not amount to £5, might own a rake, a shovel, two trowels, a bill-hook, three sheaf-picks, a hair sieve, a wire sieve, four ladders, a hand-barrow, two hurdles, a manger, and various coils of rope; together with an axe, a hatchet, two augers, a handsaw, a hammer, a pair of puncheons, and a crowbar—equipment which would not shame the tool-shed of a modern, suburban, middle-class, do-it-himself, commuter intent on injecting physical weekend meaning into an impalpable workday life-style.

Everitt thus makes a case for the variety, and sometimes the skill, of farmwork. He fails, however, to discuss its hardship. Moreover, he detects, even by the early seventeenth century, a changing attitude of employers towards labourers. In place of the semi-feudal, patriarchal relationship of the past, there was developing a 'commercial nexus between masters and men': 'farmworkers were ceasing to be thought of as respected members of a distinct social order, with peculiar rights and privileges of their own; they were coming to be regarded, instead, as a class of pariahs, and spoken of collectively, and a little condescendingly, as "the poor"'. 'It would not be many years', adds Everitt, 'before they were described as the "rude forefathers of the hamlet"'—nor before Martha Finney of Fulshaw said, in the 1760s, 'the poor people are all vile Rogues & thieves'. On the job-satisfactions and the intimate social relationships of the uneven past we need more light.

Beneath the surface of the community an immense and hidden life has always throbbed, leaving a fragile resonance in the interstices of archives, in letters, diaries, and photographs, in newspaper reports and interviews, in personal reminiscences and folk memory. From this vast sea of vanished life the historian preserves a trickle. Sometimes shells remain that housed this patient life—the tiny front room of the miner's house, for instance, in which six miners lowered the body of William Morel gently on to six chairs. And outside is the scarred landscape. After the untold lives of ordinary people the landscape is the most pervasive feature of local life, a palimpsest of a country's history. Sometimes, and particularly today, the shallow evidence of the past has been excised completely, but often—in the country and in quiet corners of towns—trees, hedges, buildings, speak to the looking eye. Increasingly, roads are made for cars, and we miss the sense of belonging that walking gives. But, informed by documents and maps, old men's tales, and above all by the second look, we can find archaic paths, walk over ancient fields, follow immemorial river banks, even make across freshly built housing estates, and still see the imprint of vanished generations.

Topographically, Wilmslow is interesting because, in a way which seems characteristic of east Cheshire, widely separated hamlets developed independently, and then united as townships of an extensive parish: Chorley, Dean Row, Fulshaw, Hough, Morley, Styal, the centre of the village itself. Where a hamlet remained physically distinct and relatively undeveloped a local community spirit survived; where it spread and became built over this spirit largely disappeared.

The centre of Wilmslow has suffered more than any other part from the changes of the last hundred years. In 1851 twenty per cent (968) of the total population (4,952) of Wilmslow lived in nine central streets: Chancel Lane, Bridge Foot, Church Street, Grove Street, Parsonage Green, Green Lane, Swan Street, Manchester Road, and Mill Lane. Today these streets have a population of, say, a hundred, or less than 0.4 per cent of the whole population of Wilmslow. Church Street has fared worst of all: today it has many empty spaces, and only a handful of buildings that recall the traditional character of what was once the principal street of the village. In 1851 Church Street had a population of 287, including shopkeepers, weavers, agricultural labourers, innkeepers, farmers, and a doctor. Today it has eight lived-in houses, and a population that must be less than thirty.

As Wilmslow grew and the resident population drained away from the centre, Church Street decayed and Grove Street became the lively focus of the town. In 1851 Grove Street had a population of 92, only five of them shopkeepers. Today the street is all shops, has a resident adult population of less than twenty, and exhibits a fast-changing façade of architectural styles from the early 19th century to the current year.

Since 1851 practically all the working class population of the central area has disappeared—the families of the 56 cotton and silk workers, the 21 agricultural labourers, the 27 journeyman craftsmen. They were concentrated in the oldest quarters of the village: Chancel Lane, Bridge Foot, Mill Lane, the bottom end of Church Street, Parsonage Green, and Green Lane. Not only have most of their houses gone but, in some cases—for instance, Bridge Foot—the very memory of the existence of a community has virtually vanished. The middle class, too, has largely gone from this central district—the families of the eight master craftsmen, five farmers, five land proprietors, three house proprietors, four doctors, four school-teachers, and thirty-seven shopkeepers.

Of these central streets Manchester Road (south of the Bollin) has the largest resident population compared with 1851: 174 residents then, about fifty today. In 1851 the street had a wide social spread: twenty-two working class families, six shopkeepers, two schoolteachers, a doctor, a manufacturer, a merchant, a land proprietor, a house proprietor, a farmer, an innkeeper. One suspects that still today it has the widest social spectrum of the central area.

In the last hundred years or so, therefore, the old centre of Wilmslow has lost a good deal of its historic and social character. Nevertheless, in spite of drainage of population and demolition of buildings, there still remain elements of this character:

the juxtaposition of St. Bartholomew's and the George and Dragon, the occasional old houses in Church Street and Swan Street, the narrowness of Grove Street, and the late 18th century houses in Manchester Road which retain traces of the conjunction of residence and small industry once characteristic of much of Wilmslow. The street pattern, too, although increasingly altered to suit modern needs, still preserves its basic historic shape: Chancel Lane bending round to mount the hill, the triangular broadening of Church Street at its foot (originally to accommodate the village market?), Green Lane, the old curving route through the village, and Grove Street and Manchester Road, the straight turnpike roads cut in the late 18th century.

Although no doubt considerably altered over the years, the Bollin valley still retains interesting traces of the various stages of its past. Historically, the crossing of the Bollin is the most significant point in Wilmslow, because the rising ground immediately south of the river is likely to have been the site of the original Anglo-Saxon settlement, and nearby the Fittons built the headquarters of their medieval estate. This significance is witnessed today by St. Bartholomew's, by vestiges of Bollin Hall (a large barn, and the old approach to the Hall across the river), and by remains of the village corn mill—the lade, and the shell of the mill itself. On the other side of the road, the Carrs, by their name and their feel, hint at their ancient role of village pasture land, and the lines of trees that approach and cross them speak of division into fields, inclusion in old estates, and transitory industrial uses.

The historical interest of the Bollin valley intensifies again at Styal. Styal is important both for its mill and its village; and the village is interesting both for the houses which the Gregs built in association with their mill, and for the much older buildings like Oak Farm which are the remains of an earlier, agricultural community. There is testimony in the name of one of the fields—Town Field—to the existence at Styal of open-field farming, of which there is otherwise little evidence in this part of Cheshire.

In 1842 Fulshaw was a largely open, rural township, with eight scattered farms, and the main group of houses concentrated on Fulshaw cross. Half of the land was owned by the lord of the manor. In addition to the eight farmers there were thirty smallholders with less than fifteen acres each, and eighteen cottagers. In 1851 Fulshaw had a total population of 358; eighty-five per cent (151) of those employed were working class or craftsmen, over one-third of them handloom weavers, and over one-quarter agricultural labourers. Only fifteen per cent (24) were middle class, including two merchants and one manufacturer. The advent of the railway in the mid-nineteenth century profoundly changed the social character and physical appearance of Fulshaw, bringing a new middle class to live in large Victorian mansions. These houses, with their extensive gardens, still characterise the area, but are increasingly challenged by modern middle class houses. Dotted among later property can still be found some of the old farm buildings of the earlier Fulshaw, now converted to white-painted private houses. Only two working farms remain.

Lindow Moss was once an enormous area stretching from Water Lane and Hawthorn Street on the east to Lindow End in the south-west. Burdett's map of 1777 shows it to have been, along with the River Bollin, the dominant geographical feature of Wilmslow. A great deal of peaty moss, unlikely to be built on, remains, but the area has been much encroached on, by building at the eastern edge, and by farms on the south and west. In the heart of the Moss still exist ancient small farms such as Saltersley and Hollingee (both just in Mobberley); a small number of private moss rooms remain, but intensive commercial cutting of peat has recently begun, and one part of the Moss is used as a council tip.

How much of the physical past should we preserve? The director of a regional civic trust, dissociating himself from 'militant conservationist pressure groups', sees the need for 'a meeting of minds' between preservationists and developers: furtherance of the quality of life may mean radical modernisation and development, 'but cities live by change' and will die without it. An architect sees some local preservationists as 'a crowd of amateurs playing at architects . . . creating a form of mass hysteria when, in fact, what we need is a group of gifted professionals supported by an intellectual patronage as in the Victorian era, capable of distinguishing what should be conserved and using it'.

Certainly, the present is getting rid of the past more quickly than ever before. The chairman of a preservationist society claims that his city has 'not seen a destruction comparable to what is now taking place since it was bombed in the last war', with 'relatively unselective' demolition involving the 'irreplaceable loss of valuable buildings'. In the pre-industrial past houses were often added to (like Preston Cottage), adapted (like White Hall—from manor house to tenant farm), or clad in modern dress (like Dukenfield Hall, Mobberley, a cruck house sheathed in Jacobean brick). Even when the modern age began, historic houses could be demolished with apparently little register (recollections of Bollin Hall's appearance before its displacement by the railway were various), perhaps because the past was seemingly inexhaustible. Now, in city centres and flush suburbs, there is an urge to sever most of the ancestral cords. Substantial eighteenth century mansions like Wilmslow's old rectory become 'eye-sores'; Georgian terraces like Manchester Road are dismissed as 'Victorian rubbish'; solid Victorian homes like River Street are condemned as 'surely our district's nearest approach to squalor'.

However, there is evidence of backlash against the demolishers: schemes 'carried out with the aid of repair and improvement grants' show 'the financial as well as the human and architectural advantages of restoration'; 'rehabilitation is a good way of retaining life in an urban area'. Of course, a house can be preserved as a building, yet lose the surroundings which gave it context; or have its exterior academically restored, yet be internally unrecognizable. Nevertheless, there is an emotional quality which only old buildings can give to urban and suburban life: without the depth of retrospect we lose a fourth dimension. Above all, houses are the matrixes of human beings: even the sharp, time-shorn buildings we raise today will belong tomorrow to the past, and become the quiet memorials of our own hidden lives.

For Pat

Acknowledgment

To some extent the pattern of this book has been dictated by the illustrations that are available. The idea for it was first suggested by the wonderfully evocative picture (4) of farmworkers crossing the Bollin. This is one of a number of sepia prints (1, 4, 5, 7, 13, 32, 33, 44, 45) of the same period which are now in Wilmslow Library. Also there, are negatives of five views (18, 19, 31, 37, 51) by R. Bradshaw, a fine amateur photographer who not only included in his landscape the very desirable element of figures (not always welcomed by postcard manufacturers, however: they excised the man and three boys in the foreground when reproducing Bradshaw's view of Grove Street, 18) but imbued them with the gentle air of mystery which suggests that in the study of the local past two and two do not necessarily make a simple four. Wilmslow Library also made available the prints of 8, 12, 16, 21, 22, 24, 25, 27, 59, and the photolithographs for 6, 9, and 46. I am grateful to the Cheshire County Library for permission to reproduce these illustrations, and to successive Wilmslow Librarians, Mr. M. Garratt and Miss D. Westhead, for their unfailing kindness in making them accessible to me.

Other institutions which gave me generous access to illustrations, documents, and maps in their possession, and kindly allowed me to reproduce some of them here, are: the Cheshire Record Office (15, 60; 6″ O.S. map, sheet XXVIII N.W., 1911), the Lancashire Record Office (2), the National Trust, through the courtesy of Mr. J.D. Brierley (39), the Textile Council (38, 40, 41), and Wilmslow Parochial Church Council, through the courtesy of Mr. L. Doxey (10).

I am equally indebted to owners of private family collections of illustrations: to Mr. W.H. Aston (25″ O.S. plan sheet XXVIII 5, 1872), Miss B. Dearden, through the courtesy of Mrs. M. Dawson (58), Mr. A.M. Flanagan (43), Captain C.D.M. Keyworth (28), Mr. S.D. Lomas (20), Miss M. Ollerenshaw, from the collection of her brother, Mr. F. Ollerenshaw (11, 14), Mrs. V. Rahim, with the permission of Mr. D. Cobb (26), Mr. L. Statham (55), and Mr. Alan Woodall (30). Finally, I was able to select sixteen further illustrations (17, 23, 29, 34-36, 42, 47-50, 52-54, 56, 57) from the rich local collection of the late Mr. W.R. Hopley, an enthusiastic member of the Wilmslow Fire Brigade, who took great pleasure in showing his photographs to all who were interested; I am indebted to his daughter, Mrs. Judyth Smith, for generous access to them.

I have had the pleasure of speaking with a number of old inhabitants of Wilmslow, and of talking to several groups of Wilmslow local history students. I am grateful to the first for the benefit of their memories about many things which might otherwise have been difficult to understand, and to the second for the opportunity to try out a good deal of what appears here. I am conscious that there will be mistakes of fact and interpretation. I apologise for factual errors, and hope they will not be too many. As regards interpretation: every man has a valid interpretation of his own past and present; one man's account of the circumstances of many men can only be a tiny attempt at comprehension; 'history is . . . necessarily subjective and individual, conditioned by the interest and vision of the historian'.

Contents

Illustrations

I · The beginnings

William's hill

If we stand today beside the Bollin, and look across to St. Bartholomew's church on its little rise (whose steepness was much reduced when the river was diverted in 1862) we are looking at the circumscribed spot which Anglo-Saxon settlers also once saw, and called Wilmslow—'William's mound'. Who William was we do not know; perhaps he was buried here. But we can be sure that this is the very site named after him because, curiously, in the earliest, thirteenth century, documents in which Wilmslow is mentioned the name is confined to the church and churchyard; the surrounding land which today we think of as Wilmslow was called Bollin Fee or manor. Although many a place-name has Anglo-Saxon origins it must be rare to be able to put one's foot with confidence on the very spot which gave it birth. Thus Fulshaw means 'foul wood', Chorley 'peasant's clearing', and Styal 'corner of land with a sty'; but it would be difficult now to point to the exact wood, the precise clearing, the one and only corner which prompted these names.

A teasing mystery, however, remains. In the early thirteenth century Sir Richard Fitton acquired the lordship of Fulshaw, a territory which extended from Styal in the north to Chorley in the south. Soon afterwards his son, also Richard, gave the manor (a small part of the lordship) of Fulshaw to the knights of St. John of Jerusalem, and about the same time is referred to as lord of Bollin. From the charters recording these transactions an interesting deduction appears valid. It looks as though, in the beginning, it was Fulshaw which was the heartland of this domain, not the site by the river which seems to us so naturally the centre of old Wilmslow. It was only when the Fittons gave Fulshaw to the knights of St. John and moved their headquarters from the hinterland to the banks of the Bollin that Wilmslow began to have both documentary and physical existence. Bollin Hall, St. Bartholomew's, and the earliest houses around them, must all have been built in this period, the second quarter of the thirteenth century. How then did the name 'Wilmslow', apparently originating in Anglo-Saxon times, manage to survive, say, four or five hundred years, to emerge as the style of a nascent hamlet in the thirteenth century?

1. St. Bartholomew's from Chancel Lane bridge

A seven hundred years-old stream

'Let all men, present and to come, know that I, Robert, son of Mathew of Fulshaw, have given, granted, and by this my present charter have confirmed to lord Richard Fyton, knight, all my fee of Fulshaw, namely Fulshaw, Chorley, Pownall, Morley, with all my land of Ullerswood, namely as far as the mid-stream of the siche which comes from the Black Lake of Shadow Moss, and so descending the siche till it falls into the Bollin, with Styal, Curbishley, Northcliffe, Rylands, Stanneylands, and Harethorn, and all the lordship pertaining to the said fee'.

This document—undated, but, according to Earwaker, c.1200—is the, so-to-speak, foundation charter of Wilmslow. It is intriguing that Wilmslow itself is not mentioned, but it is also, as Earwaker points out, 'particularly interesting as showing how many of the names still in existence in the parish have been handed down from very early times'. Closer examination reveals that the charter deals with a broad band of territory embracing the later townships of Chorley, Fulshaw, and Pownall, embedded in which are the settlements of Styal, Curbishley, Norcliffe, Rylands, Stanneylands, and Hawthorn. What is noticeable about this catalogue of names is that it excludes the whole of the eastern side of Wilmslow parish, namely that part soon to be called Bollin Fee with its constituent townships of Hough and Dean Row: it seems clear that Bollin Fee was not part of the lordship of Fulshaw, and that it was only when the Fittons moved from Fulshaw to the banks of the Bollin in the mid-thirteenth century that Bollin Fee became an identifiable part of the Wilmslow area.

'. . . all my fee . . . as far as the mid-stream of the siche which comes from the Black Lake of Shadow Moss, and so descending the siche till it falls into the Bollin . . .'. In discussing this charter Earwaker says that the 'siche' (a small stream) is 'not now recognisable'. However, if one looks at a map of the area drawn before the construction of Ringway airport (for instance, Greenwood's map of Cheshire, 1819, or Swire and Hutching's map of Cheshire, 1828-9) a stream flowing from Shadow Moss to the Bollin is clearly in evidence. For two-thirds of its distance—from the Moss to Higher Mainwood Farm—it coincides with the parish and the urban district boundaries, then branches off northwards, through Cotteril Clough, to the Bollin.

2. Grant by Robert, son of Mathew of Fulshaw, to Sir Richard Fitton of his fee of Fulshaw, c. 1200?

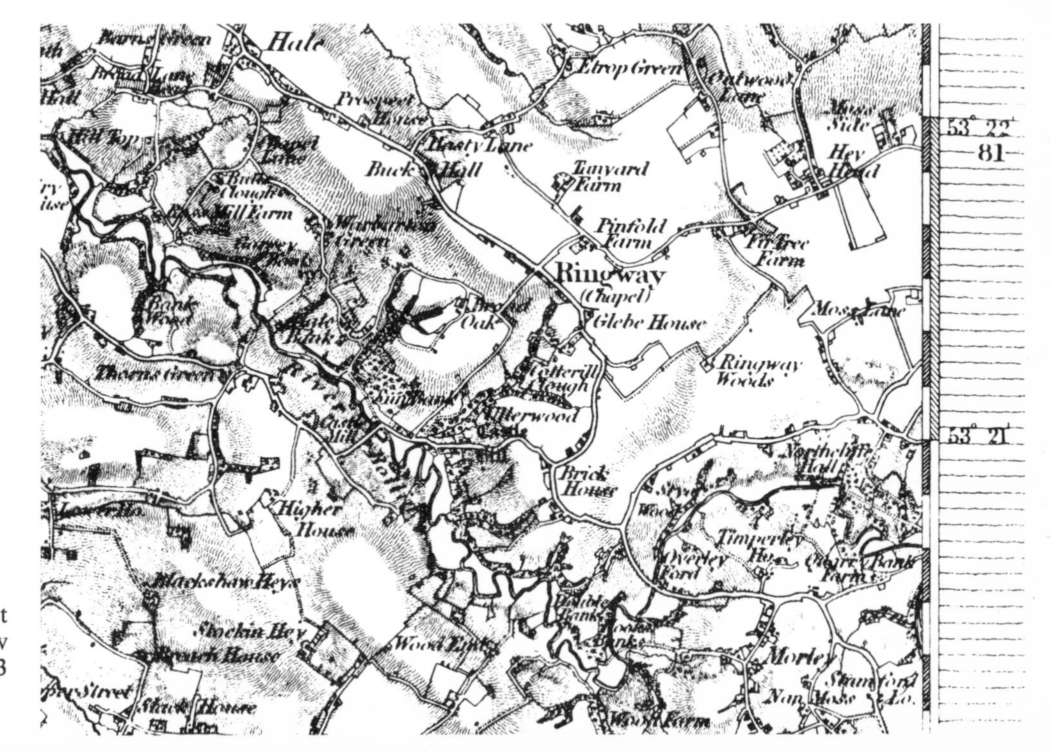

3. The north-west boundary of Wilmslow near Ringway, 1842–3

It is interesting that this tenurial boundary of nearly eight hundred years ago became, at some unknown date, largely the boundary also of Wilmslow parish; and that the piece of territory between Oversleyford and Cotteril Clough, which is excluded from the parish, should be identifiable (and is so identified by the first edition of the 1″ Ordnance Survey) as that Ullerswood which Robert of Fulshaw in his charter somehow distinguishes from 'all my fee of Fulshaw'.

Bridge across the Bollin

Two men, two boys, a horse, a cart, and a farm dog pause to have their photographs taken as they make the crossing of the river Bollin one spring morning half a century ago. The horse, the cart, the dress of the men, the *stillness* of the photograph tie the scene to England's historic rural past, which died in the nineteenth century, but whose ghost was successfully exorcized only by the second world war.

The bridge they are crossing and the road they are treading, also, are historic. There have clearly been two bridges here: a stone one, leaving substantial well-made buttresses, and a later wooden one with the unsophisticated air of a poor inheritor. The route, which has now completely gone, was in fact one of the principal medieval ways into and out of Wilmslow. Its position was dictated by the site of Bollin Hall, the home of the Fittons who came here in the early thirteenth century, built the church, and dominated the hamlet which began to straggle up the hill from the river.

The 6″ Ordnance Survey map of 1930–45 shows the wooden bridge still in existence, as well as the road which led across it to Dean Row and ultimately to Stockport. Today, north of the bridge, this road is choked with bushes, but on the south side it still reaches, unused, for the vanished manorial hall which it once served.

4. Bollin Hall Farm bridge

Bollin Hall

Horse and cart, having crossed the Bollin, and passed up the lane which, cambered and metalled beneath untrodden grass, still runs between its hawthorn hedges, pose outside a barn of Bollin Hall Farm. It is a pity that the photographer did not afterwards swing his camera once more to the right, to show us the farm which replaced the medieval hall: did it incorporate anything of its predecessor? A lot depends on the precise situation of the old hall.

Although the 25″ O.S. plan of 1872 appears to show the medieval route across the river pointing straight at a house centrally sited among outbuildings, Andrew Pearson, writing in 1897, insists that the 'present Hall and buildings' were only erected 'near to the old site', and that the old hall, which was taken down to make way for the railway in 1842, stood where the south end of the viaduct now stands. Pearson could just remember it as, rather surprisingly, 'a plain, substantial brick building with outbuildings to match', old-fashioned dove-cotes, and, 'if tradition be correct . . . formerly an old Norman Chapel connected with it'. Earwaker, too, had it described to him as 'a square brick building of considerable size, and showing signs of having been at one time a very important place, as there were remains of extensive gardens round it'. William Norbury, on the other hand, remembered it as 'something like Chorley Hall, an old framed building'. So far no map has been found which shows Bollin Hall intact before the construction of the railway, nor any picture of either hall or farm.

Two features which do appear clearly in the photograph are the old road leading away eastwards across the Bollin, and the mill lane, surprisingly full and deceptively broad, flowing from its weir half a mile up the river down to the wheel of Wilmslow's corn mill near Manchester Road.

5. Barn and mill lade near Bollin Hall Farm

II · The centre

Church and village

A manor house will last you seven hundred years, a parish church a good deal longer. Nothing intrinsic remains of the mysterious medieval hall which decided the existence of Wilmslow, but the church which the Fittons created endures, many-pictured. A third member of the old community has also gone—the people's houses which once clustered round the church, penning a narrow cemetery against its flanks.

Keyworth's pleasant drawing of Wilmslow's backs shows St. Bartholomew's rising on its hill above trees, houses, and river, with an unusual glimpse of the homes on Chancel Lane which were taken down a generation ago to widen the ancient narrow street. Though old, these houses were substantial, with stone roofs. More flimsy, more archaic cottages had gone earlier, in 1829 and 1862, to enlarge a tiny graveyard of 2,270 square yards. The extension of 1829 added 772 square yards in a strip stretching from the church gate to the river. The addition of 1862 was much bigger—between five and six thousand square yards—and involved not only the demolition of hearse house and cottages, but the removal of 6,000 cartloads of soil in order to shift the bed of the Bollin away from the church.

We are fortunate in having a description, in Fryer's *Wilmslow graves*, of all these clustering cottages as they existed about 1820. There were then about seventeen, strung in three-quarters of a circle between church gate and Chancel Lane. They were all thatched, mainly one-storeyed, and occupied by small people like handloom weavers, a shopkeeper, the sexton, John Gibbin, 'a quack doctor, who was frequently absent. His wife gained a little money by providing accommodation for lodgers', and Ellen Henshall—'poor old Ellen lived by herself in one of the rooms, as her son had unfortunately been concerned in the riots, and was far away over sea. The further apartment she let to old John Beard for a warping-room'. By 1851 the houses had been reduced to a dozen on the west and north sides of the church, but the social composition was much the same as in 1820: a master joiner employing one man, four cotton handloom weavers, a silk throwster, a tailor, a bricklayer, a farmer of six acres, and a bailiff.

6. St. Bartholomew's and the back of Chancel Lane, 1889

St. Bartholomew's

A church belonging to the manor of Bollin, and probably recently completed by the Fittons, is first mentioned in 1264, but we know nothing of its appearance. There is a crypt beneath the present chancel which is likely to belong to a previous building, and the base of the tower may be fifteenth century; the bulk of the fabric, however, dates from a rebuilding in the early sixteenth century during the rectorship (1517–37) of Henry Trafford. Trafford appears to have been responsible for the very handsome wooden ceiling over both nave and chancel: his initials can be seen on some of the bosses. He is credited with building, or rebuilding, the chancel, but it is odd that, before the roof of the chancel was raised in 1897–8, its ceiling ran two feet below the point of the east window arch. Fryer points to what appear to be sharply inclined roof marks on the wall above the arch at the west end of the nave, which conform closely with the pitch of the chancel gable as it was in his time, and so suggest that the nave was once the same height as the chancel.

The present appearance of the church owes a lot to restorations which followed

7. St. Bartholomew's: interior before the restoration of 1862

faculties obtained in 1862 and 1897: a new vestry was built on the north side; the west door was first opened, then closed, as the main entrance to the church; the south porch was demolished and reconstructed; the pinnacles of the tower, erected in 1636, were taken down and rebuilt; the hearse house which jutted out into Chancel Lane was removed; the churchyard wall was refashioned and a lychgate provided; and the characteristic quirk in the roof line was ironed out by raising the chancel. These alterations, together with changes inside the building, finally severed the church, ecclesiastically, from its medieval past. The transformation which ended its physical setting at the centre of an ancient village community was the great extension of the churchyard in 1862 which involved not only manhandling the bed of the river Bollin, but demolishing the cottages, and stopping the way, which together had embraced the church on its western and northern sides.

In 1862 St. Bartholomew's suffered what has been described as a 'disastrous restoration'. It is agreed that the church was in urgent need of repair: in 1835 a box was bought 'for the minister to stand on in wet weather'; and later 'the flooring of the pews generally was so rotten that a careless footstep would have plunged into the coffins of the dead, which were in several instances within a few inches of the bottom of pews'. A faculty of 17 July 1862 provided for removing coffins and corpses from the north transept, levelling the floor, and installing underfloor heating. But the restoration involved other alterations which a later generation was to find inexcusable, including the 'wanton destruction' of the old pews.

Before the Reformation there were few pews in the church, 'and those belonged to the principal inhabitants'. From the mid-seventeenth century, however, other families followed suit, and most of the nave filled up with seating. By the mid-nineteenth century 'the effect of looking down from the galleries upon the pewed floor was at once painful and ludicrous . . . by their resemblance to the irregular appearance of a child's puzzle'. Aisles varied in width, the centre one being sometimes seven, sometimes only three feet wide. The pews were of all shapes and sizes, 'very many of them being only two feet three inches wide, so that it was utterly impossible to kneel, or even to sit in them with any degree of comfort'. One pew was set aside for the poor, 'and this in the coldest and most remote part'.

Other features excited the distaste of eighteenth and nineteenth century reformers. Above the rood screen a lath and plaster partition descended from the ceiling between chancel and nave, obscuring the light from the east window. On it were a 'wretched gross Daubing of Moses and Aaron with his Fool's Bells standing on each side the tables of the Decalogue' and 'tawdry Garlands of Tinsel and painted Paper'. There were 'grotesque decorations', too, over the arches of the nave and at the west end, while other wall paintings had been covered with plaster, 'as if to increase the gloom and disfigurement of the church'. The restoration of 1862–63 got rid of both plaster and paintings beneath. It also removed the lath and plaster partition, and replaced it by 'a lofty, modern chancel arch', but, because of the lowness of the chancel, the arch was 'unpleasantly cut across' by a two-foot depth of chancel ceiling. The intrusive south gallery was taken down; and the ornate pulpit, bought in 1639 and 'beautified' with carving in 1640, was displaced.

Further drastic restoration of the church was carried out following a faculty of 28 October 1897. The most dramatic aspect was reconstruction of the chancel: raising its roof and east window, inserting a clerestory, and erecting a new reredos. But the most controversial feature was 'mutilation' of the screens erected in the sixteenth century. The rood screen suffered most: 'there are now only a few scraps of the old wood left, and the proportions have been considerably altered'; it was even 'subjected to the indignity of a rood loft (with no means of access)', but this was removed about 1936. The screens separating the aisles from the north and south chapels had crestings added to them, but money ran out before the same could be done to those dividing chapels from chancel, so these are almost in their original state, 'ending in the simple and dignified brestsummer board'.

The old rectory?

In this apparently little house, the home in the early part of this century of Daniel Sumner, boot and shoe maker, it is difficult to see the lineaments of a rectory, or the setting of a siege during the civil war in which the rector was captured by a par-

8. St. Bartholomew's: interior before the restoration of 1897

liamentary force and one or two of his servants were killed. Yet there is a strong local tradition that this house was the old rectory, and an official inscription, erected when the houses in Chancel Lane were demolished, commemorated it as a fact.

Certainly, closer investigation reveals a bigger building than appears at first sight: the brick house on the right has been built against its face (or rear), masking a dormer gable; and the 25″ O.S. plan of 1872 confirms a long building with its main axis at right angles to Chancel Lane (into which it juts), and out of line with the rest of the younger buildings in the street. Yet a house worthy of siege in a civil war surely needs to have been much bigger still. That in fact it was so is demonstrated by the probate inventory of Thomas Wright, the rector who suffered the attack, and who died in 1661. The inventory not only discloses a house of twenty-one rooms—easily one of the biggest in Wilmslow—but mentions a gatehouse. The impression of size is reinforced by a terrier of the rectory in 1663 which describes a house of five bays with, in addition, 'buildings about the inner court' of five and a half bays, and barns, a cowhouse, and other outbuildings totalling fourteen bays; there were also an orchard and a garden adjoining the house, and a field of two acres next to them. Clearly, the rectory was not only a considerable building; it was built round a courtyard and had a gatehouse, in the style of a large manor house.

That the rectory of 1663 was not on Chancel Lane is clinched by a description in the terrier of the boundaries of the two-acre field which lay near to it, and by the name of the field. It was a close called Kirkcroft, bounded on the north by 'the lane leading betwixt Wilmslow and the Hough'. This points conclusively to the site at Parsonage Green which is occupied by the present 'old rectory'; Cowcroft, the name today of the lane which runs outside its wall, is clearly a corruption of Kirkcroft. We know that the present rectory at Parsonage Green was completed in 1778 by the Rev. Edward Beresford; he built it because, as he reported to his bishop, the existing building was 'in such bad condition as to make it necessary to pull it quite down and to build an entire new house'. How long, then, had a rectory been there? How old, in effect, is the name Parsonage Green?

There is some evidence that the earliest, medieval, rectory was near the west end of the church, in what is now the churchyard. Was the 'old rectory' on Chancel Lane an intermediate rectory between the medieval one and the rectory at Parsonage Green? The house of Henry Trafford, rector between 1542 and 1591, must have been substantial because he had six servants and a farm which included six oxen and twenty-one cows. On the other hand his inventory lists only eight beds and his will mentions only three rooms—hall, buttery, and kitchen. Perhaps such a house, standing alone, could be fitted into the site on Chancel Lane? Earwaker evidently thought so: 'There is a tradition that the old gabled house to the east of the church, and which projects out into the road, was the old parsonage; of the truth of this tradition no evidence has occurred. The highroad separates it from the churchyard. There are remains of an old buttery, etc.; all the tokens of a house of some pretensions'.

9. Chancel Lane, c.1889

An array of Bowers

In the early thirteenth century Richard Fitton, knight, moved his capital messuage from the heartland of Fulshaw to the banks of the Bollin, where he created a fresh estate, built a new church, and began the physical development of Wilmslow. Five and a half centuries later Ralph Bower, yeoman, moved an embryonic cotton factory from the hinterland of Chorley to a site a quarter of a mile away from the remains of Bollin Hall, bought houses, built mills, acquired a landed estate, and began the industrial development of Wilmslow. The manorial power of the Fittons and the commercial sway of the Bowers have both gone and are forgotten, but each helped to mould the Wilmslow we know today.

In the eighteenth century Ralph Bower (whose ancestors must have been Cheshire bow makers) was a farmer at Blackshaw's i' th' Fields behind Chorley Hall. We know of an earlier Ralph Bower of Chorley who was a miller, owned houses in Macclesfield, and when he died in 1763 left most of his estate to Peter Pimlott, a Fulshaw weaver who had gone to London. This Ralph's stepmother, Sarah, died in 1766 and left all her household goods to William, Matthew, and Sarah, the children of Matthew Bower the elder of Chorley, husbandman; to Martha Legh, wife of William Legh of Warford, yeoman, she left £5 and 'my dark coloured camblet gown, cloak, pair of stays, red silk handkerchief, and pair of gloves'; to their son, William Legh, she left one book, 'A Compleat Christian Dictionary'.

Ralph Bower the farmer had a large family—six sons and three daughters; possibly to employ them he began spinning cotton (which was then superseding the spinning of wool in the Wilmslow neighbourhood) in his home. A little before 1787, catching the spirit of the times ushered in by the inventions and enterprise of Arkwright, Hargreaves, and Crompton, he migrated from the old farm at Chorley to a new house at Wilmslow, and built on the Bollin a small factory with a water wheel, to carry out the preliminary processes of carding and slubbing.

We can be pretty sure where Ralph Bower's house was in Wilmslow: next but one to the church (Fryer says his 'ancestor's' initials, BCB 1764, were still on the wall in 1886, but one would like to think they really read R(alph)(and)C(atharine)B(ower) 1784). There is some doubt, however, where his mill lay. William Norbury says confidently that, known as 'the new building', it was the factory which subsequently became Barber's silk mill in the Carrs. Samuel Finney, however, puts it 'on the Bolin, near Wilmslow bridge', a site which plausibly coincides with Fryer's description of the churchyard: 'entering the gates and keeping to the left . . . then came an opening which led down to a little mill some thirty yards in length belonging to Lownds Bower . . . The depression by the river in which the mill stood was called the Folly Holes . . . The mill barred the way at the bottom'. The surveyor's plan of 1822 for the extension of the churchyard bears out Fryer's description, and the building-block adjacent to the words 'River Bollin' looks a likely candidate for Bower's mill, although its dimensions do not appear to tally with Fryer's 'thirty yards in length'.

The sequence of industrialists who came to Wilmslow in the 1780s is difficult to

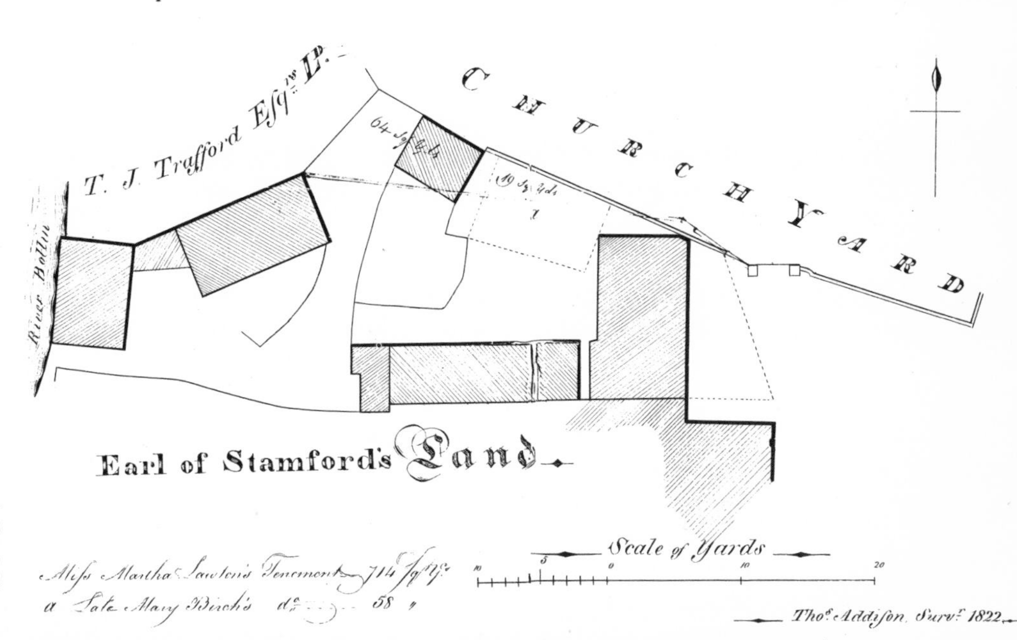

10. Plan of St. Bartholomew's churchyard extension, 1822

establish, but by 1787 there were 'about one hundred and fifty employed . . . in and about Wilmslow, in Picking, Carding, and Slubbing Cotton, and Spinning the same into Yarn under four or five Masters', and 'Mr. Bower' was 'one of the most Capital Masters in this branch'. When he died in 1801 Ralph Bower, cotton merchant, had done well. He left his wife, Catharine, 'a small settlement . . . out of an estate or tenement in Chorley called the Fields', and also all his 'dwelling house and premises in Hough called Leicester's Tenement . . . during her life in case she shall not marry again and conduct herself in a decent and proper manner'. All the rest of his estate he left, share and share alike, to his sons and daughters; and this was extensive: in addition to his factory there was Hawthorn estate which he bought about 1800 and which then extended from the Bollin to Parsonage Green. 'His many sons grew up, and each in his turn became a spinner or manufacturer, and soon Wilmslow became noted for its cotton shops'.

When the little mill on the Bollin disappeared is not clear; it was still there c. 1816–26. Perhaps it was removed by the churchyard extension of 1829; if not then, certainly by the much bigger extension of 1862, when the river was bodily lifted out of the channel which gave the mill its power. This historic site must now be sought in the south-west corner of the churchyard: the old has been swallowed by the ancient.

William Bower, 1801–1862

When Ralph, the founder of the industrial dynasty of Bowers, died in 1801 he divided his empire equally among his six sons, William, Charles, Ralph, Lowndes, Warburton, and John; and his three daughters, Nancy, Catharine, and Jane. Unfortunately, the full extent and details of this patrimony are not yet clear. From what Fryer says, the cotton mill on the Bollin went to Lowndes. Charles, who died 'cotton spinner' in 1806, left his estate to be sold for the maintenance of his children. William was described as gentleman at his death in 1827; he had received the Grove part of the Hawthorn estate from his father, and he now left £1,000 each to his daughters, Ann and Isabella, and the residue to them and his son George. John, 'landed proprietor', died in 1853, aged seventy-two. He lived in a house at the corner of Manchester Road and Mill Brow, and had a daughter, Elizabeth, and two sons, John, who was a corn dealer and draper, and Elijah, an artist. To John he left his house; to Elijah, Dunge Fold Fields with the house on them and £700; to Elizabeth, £500 and an annuity 'issuing out of my share of the silk mill or factory in Wilmslow in the holding of Mr. Charles Barber'. Ralph, gentleman, of Hawthorn Hall, died in 1834 and left the longest will of any of the Bowers. Its most significant item was the bequest of 'all and singular the steam engines, boilers, machinery, wheels, mill gearing, going gear, utensils, and implements of trade which shall be in my cotton mill or factory in Wilmslow or used in the trade or business now carried on there by my son William to him for his absolute use'.

11. William Bower

This William is the best known member of the Bower family. The site of his steam mill can be found from the tithe award map of 1840 which shows it to have been on Mill Lane, now occupied by a terrace of six houses of mid-nineteenth century appearance facing the garden of remembrance. About 1849 he became bankrupt, and the census of 1851 describes him as a retail grocer. In Bagshaw's *Cheshire directory* of 1850 appears a note that 'the cotton mill had been closed a few months when we visited Wilmslow'. According to Andrew Pearson, 'when Lord Stamford sold his Wilmslow Estate in the year 1857, a large portion was purchased by the late J.C. Prescott . . . who occupied the position of lord of the Bollin Manor, and he being anxious to make Wilmslow a purely residential district, bought the old cotton mill . . . with its tall chimney and had them taken down'. But it was the opinion of the late Mr. Frank Ollerenshaw, great-grandson of William Bower, that, apart from a portion which had been used for storing cotton, the mill was destroyed by fire.

Although William Bower's cotton mill did not survive, the memory of his enterprising spirit lived on in Wilmslow. In 1846 he built a gas works to light his mill, and supplied gas to the public at fourpence per light per week; later he introduced meters and supplied gas at eight shillings per thousand feet. According to Mr. Ollerenshaw he was also responsible for starting the gas works at Rhyl.

The enduring triangle

The triangle formed by Church Street, Mill Street, and Mill Road, is an ancient one, but difficult to interpret in detail. It seems likely that, in both cases, the mill referred to is the corn mill and not a later cotton mill: in 1663, for instance, Mill Street appears as the 'footway from Wilmslow town to Bollin mill', and Mill Road is 'Mill hill'. Of course, at this time, Manchester Road had not been made, so that Mill hill must be the old way (today called Mill Road) which curved round the south-east area of the early settlement, joined at right angles the route from the bottom of the town to Bollin Hall, and pointed straight at the corn mill. At its other end Mill hill entered Church Street, and it is perhaps not fanciful to see it as being continued on the other side of Church Street by the ancient way leading to the village pastures called Dunge

12. The corner of Mill Street and Mill Road, 1900

Fold, a name corrupted by Pearson's time, on the strength of the nearby parish lockup, into Dungeon Fold, and today refined into Dungeon Walk.

The anarchic scatter of Wilmslow's earliest houses is suggested by the crowded group of cottages which stood at the junction of Mill Street and Mill Road; like all the small houses which formerly surrounded the church, they were thatched. The site is now a shrubbery, but the houses were still standing in 1887 when the original of this illustration was painted by James Slater: Mill Street (then Mill Lane) is in the foreground; Mill Road (then Mill Brow) on the left.

On this jumbled triangle of rural streets the Bowers imposed an industrial pattern of factory buildings and cotton workers' houses. There is an uncertain tradition of several mills in the Church Street area, but only one can be clearly identified: William Bower's on Mill Street. No illustration of this factory has been found, but from the tithe award plan of 1840 and the 25″ Ordnance Survey plan of 1872 it appears to have occupied a rectangular site stretching half way along Mill Street from the corner of Church Street, and including outbuildings behind. It had a tall chimney whose position is unknown.

By 1850 the mill had closed and shortly afterwards it was either demolished or burned down. Part of the site on Mill Street was quickly built over with a terrace of six houses which still stand. A substantial portion at the corner of Church Street appears to have remained until 1901 when the present three houses with shops were built. A third long section at the rear of the houses in Mill Street survived until the 1920s. According to Mr. Frank Ollerenshaw this last part of the mill had been used for storing cotton. It afterwards became a lodging house whose end just appears on the right of the illustration.

Cornelius Sherriffe

Cornelius Sherriffe was an Italian rag and bone man who sold second-hand clothing in a shop at the bottom of Church Street, and used to sit in a chair by his open door. You could get good clothes there, and the shoes on his stall were 'all clean and ready'. On 20 September 1901 his shop was teetering to its close: that day he wrote to 'Messrs John Walsh and others my landlords', 'Gentlemen, In consideration of your allowing me to remain in occupation of your cottage in Church Street, Wilmslow, although my tenancy has expired, at the same rent as heretofore, I agree to give up possession after the receipt of one week's notice to do so from you'. 'Messrs John Walsh and others' were the churchwardens of St. Bartholomew's. Two years later Cornelius Sherriffe's shop was demolished.

A house next to a church is on a sensitive spot. In the case of Wilmslow the site was particularly vulnerable because of the exigencies of the graveyard. Before 1829 this was a quarter of its present size, and was pinned, from the south-west to the north-east, between the church and a semi-circle of houses which was only sixteen yards away from the west porch. In 1829, 'by reason of the great increase of parishioners in the parish of Wilmslow', the churchyard had its first extension: a bill-hook shaped piece of land of 772 square yards curling round the south-west corner.

This expansion involved the demolition of a shop with two bow windows occupied by William and Sarah Lawton, 'a worthy couple who, though dwelling within the shadow of the church, were diligent attenders of the Friends' meeting at Morley'. Next door to the Lawtons' was a building as significant in its way as Bollin Hall—

13. The bottom end of Church Street

the home of the family which brought the industrial revolution to Wilmslow. The alterations of 1829 left it standing next to the churchyard. In 1841 it was occupied by William Bower, master cotton spinner, his wife, eight children, and four relatives and servants. Next door, in a house also owned by Bower, lived James Bayley, an agricultural labourer, his wife, and three children. Next door again was the Old George Inn.

It is clear from the 25″ O.S. plan of 1872 that these two Bower houses were considerable buildings, but by the end of the nineteenth century The George and Dragon Inn had acquired their rear portions, leaving their fronts as cottages with shops. In 1896 St. Bartholomew's bought the strip of land which lay behind the Bowers' house for further addition to the churchyard. In 1900 the Cornbrook brewery acquired the two cottages and in 1903 pulled them down. The last Bower to live in this memorable house (by then known as Laurel House) was Ralph, who died in 1900. The other house was occupied by Cornelius Sherriffe, wardrobe dealer, who, curiously, also ran the 'Paddy Can'—the lodging house off Mill Street which had once been part of William Bower's cotton factory.

The old street

In the 1841 census the west side of Church Street is called Wilmslow Street, but the east side is called Old Street. This odd ambiguity is probably accidental, occurring because the two sides are dealt with in different sections of the return; and 'Old' is probably in contrast with 'New', that is, Manchester, Road. However, the rather intriguing implication that the houses on the east side represent a more ancient part of the village is given some credence by their violently erratic building line, compared with the much more even frontages of the west side of the street.

Of all the houses, shown in the illustration, on the east side of Church Street below the market place, only the one second from the left is still standing. But a fragment of its neighbour up the hill persists: the gable of its steeper roof, once, no doubt, clothed with thatch, continues to jut aloft, and against the house end are to be found, still in position, part of the box-work of a timber-framed cottage, with

14. The east side of Church Street

traces of wattle and daub infilling, and the notches and marks in the woodwork which helped the carpenter who erected the house to prop his corner posts and insert the rails and studs.

The street of shops and pubs

Mr. Arthur Ollerenshaw died in 1970, aged seventy-eight. He was born at 39 Church Street next door to the Ring o' Bells. His father was a butcher, 'the oldest butcher in Wilmslow'; his great-grandfather was William Bower, the master cotton spinner. Mr. Ollerenshaw himself became a carpenter with Coates', at that time the principal builders in Wilmslow, but before that he was a telegraph boy, and as a result, perhaps had a photographic recollection of every house in Church Street, every inhabitant, and every quirk in its building line. It was largely a street of small shops, with the owner living over or alongside, and pubs: Ted Griffiths, the hairdresser (haircut 2d, shave 1d, 5 Woodbines 1d; a churchwarden or clay pipe for a 'full customer'); Miss Shuttleworth, who sold household things like paraffin: she was burnt to death, Mr. Ollerenshaw found her; Antrobus's, the sweet shop (mint and lemon humbugs 8 for 1d); Ogden's clog shop (the ladies on conservative outings didn't speak to Mrs. Ogden); Chandler's (cooked foods and pickled herrings); the Ring o' Bells, where the Trafford rent dinner was held every Christmas (Mr. Ollerenshaw's father provided the meat, which was roasted at the nearby baker's) and where the stable had been used by the Manchester mail coach; and the Vine Inn, which caught fire: when the firemen called out, 'Your house is on fire', the innkeeper shouted back, 'Let it burn'. There was even a convalescent home—Owen's—again supplied with meat by Mr. Ollerenshaw's father, but it closed when Mr. Ollerenshaw was a boy.

The community street

Like some stranger-wary town of the old West, Church Street sits at high noon, withdrawn and brooding, waiting for the action to begin. The setted road curves narrowly down between blinded shops and irregularly façaded houses. There is no traffic; the pavements are almost deserted; but a tradesman in a white apron—butcher, hairdresser, cobbler?—has come out with his assistant to see what the photographer is up to. 'Church Street was a very old-fashioned street then'.

15. The Ring o'Bells, Church Street

In this illustration we sense the introspection and the self-sufficiency of the old community. Today Church Street has thirteen names on the voters' list. In 1851 it had sixty-seven families—287 people altogether, including twenty-two shopkeepers (among them, six grocers, four shoemakers, two bakers, a hairdresser, and a saddler), thirteen cotton and silk weavers, seven farm labourers, three licensed victuallers, and two farmers. But there was only one professional man—a doctor. Though a former master cotton spinner (William Bower, now become a retail grocer) still lived next door to the church, the middle classes, even in Wilmslow, had begun their historic flight from the centre.

In its present sad state Church Street is Wilmslow's most poignant remnant of an ancient past. Bollin Walk—the way between Bollin Hall and the village—must be older, but we know nothing of early houses along its route; and the narrow lane and thatched houses that once surrounded St. Bartholomew's are only a cultivated memory.

16. Top of the Town, Church Street

The toll-bar

Before 1775 the south-north route through Wilmslow ran along Green Lane, down Church Street, up Cliff Road, and so to Manchester via Lacey Green and Cheadle. In 1775 Samuel Finney, soi-disant intendant of Wilmslow, was responsible for getting a new road cut along what are now Grove Street and Manchester Road as part of the Wilmslow and Lawton turnpike; but as late as 1851 Grove Street was still known as New Road and Green Lane as Old Road.

The construction of a turnpike meant the erection of a toll-bar. This originally stood at the end of Brook Lane in Chorley, but about 1805 it was moved to the Water Lane end of Grove Street. The illustration shown here has sometimes been dated 1837, but this is not possible because the buildings depicted on the left had not been erected as late as 1860; perhaps the date should read 1873?

The Wilmslow toll-bar lasted only about seventy years. In its later days the turnpike became a source of irritation to Wilmslow inhabitants: it was run by the Highway Board, a 'band of puppets who (with a few honourable exceptions) spend an hour a month with their legs under the table in the Board Room of the Union Workhouse at Macclesfield'; and, moreover, Wilmslow people were 'taxed to maintain in repair roads around Macclesfield which they seldom or never use'.

A plot was therefore laid for 'a considerable number of the oldest established tradesmen in the town' to demolish the toll-bar with axes on the last day of the year, 1876, after a midnight procession along Grove Street to the sound of the bells of St. Bartholomew's; followed by fireworks, effigy burning, and 'a kind of celebration supper' in the Literary Institution. But in fact the tradesmen got cold feet, didn't turn up, and the large crowd dispersed after trying to pull down the bar by hand. In any case the whole demonstration was a trifle bogus: legal demolition of the toll-bar had already been arranged. The following morning workmen of Sir Humphrey de Trafford arrived to take it down: 'a barrel of ale was carried into one of the lower rooms, and from thence doled out in jugs and glasses to the multitude, who ever and anon gave three cheers for the deliverance from the bars, and three hearty groans for the Czar of the Highways fraternity'.

The late Mr. Arnold Grimshaw believed that his mother, who died aged ninety-

17. Grove Street toll-bar, before 1877

two, was probably one of the last to pay toll through the Wilmslow bar: she drove a four-wheeled phaeton and payed one shilling—threepence on each wheel. Mr. Grimshaw also identified the two-wheeled truck shown in the illustration as common in his boyhood: it was one borrowed from Lord Vernon's coal yard at the old station approach and carried a hundredweight of coal.

The Grove

Grove Street today is vigorous and volatile, a jumble of architectural styles and dissonant roof lines, its facades constantly changing under the impact of commercial flux. A century ago it was quiet and largely residential, almost unhoused on one side, its development determined by accidents of ownership and the deaths of landed proprietors.

About 1800 Ralph Bower, the thrusting yeoman farmer turned master cotton spinner, having made a fortune out of his mill on the Bollin, bought the Hawthorn estate, which stretched from Parsonage Green to Pownall Park. When he died in 1801 his lands were divided between his six sons and three daughters. William, the eldest, got an area to the west of the 'new' road, cut a generation before. Soon afterwards he built the Grove, half way along this street, as an inn and posting house. It was still an inn in 1840, occupied by Ralph Warrington: a considerable establishment with extensive outbuildings, a stockyard, an orchard, and a bowling green and garden which stretched along the middle reaches of Grove Street. But by 1851 it was lived in as a private house by the unmarried daughters of William Bower, Ann and Isabella.

The east side of Grove Street was also largely Bower land, but because no big house and grounds were involved it sprouted cottages and shops quite soon. Development of the west side, on the other hand, was arrested by the central position of the Grove: as late as 1860 there were, in addition to the Grove, only the toll-house at Water Lane corner, and, half way towards it, the modest house of William Gratrex, 'the village lawyer'. But by 1872 nine shops had been built between the toll-house and the southern corner of the Grove's bowling green, and two shops at Hawthorn Lane corner.

As can be seen from the illustration, four other houses of similar design and roof line adjoined the two at the corner of Hawthorn Lane, so it seems likely that they, too, were built about 1872; the point they reached was the north end of the Grove's garden. Development of the Grove itself had to await the deaths of the Misses Bower. About 1886 a Mr. Mark Wood bought the Grove and converted it into shops, filling the gap between house front and street line with a baroque facade. By 1898 the rest of Grove Street had been built up with shops, all with high, extravagant, late-Victorian gables. In modern times half of the Grove became a bank with living accommodation above. In 1974 this part of the oldest house in Grove Street, by now bearing practically no trace of its original character apart, perhaps, from a few cobbles and a water trough in its backyard, was demolished.

18. The north end of Grove Street

The island

An unknown man in a trilby—commercial traveller or simply on his way to the station?—walks down a sunlit, unfrequented Grove Street, his right foot for ever poised at ten-to-two outside the District Bank. There are no cars; a bicycle stands parked in the gutter against the pavement; other cycles are coming up the street, one of them precisely in the middle. A workman pushes one wheelbarrow towards another; a 'bus, curved like a coach, passes across Bank Square: the man in the trilby is walking through the shadows of trees.

The trees, and the alley the man is passing, are a reminder of the gardens which once connected Grove Street and Green Lane, across the segment which lay between the dead straight turnpike and the old curving route through Wilmslow. By 1841, though by no means thoroughly built over, this island housed a vigorous and miscellaneous community, a contrast to the staid and undeveloped stretch on the west side of the street. Admittedly, as on the west side, much of the land in the island had belonged to Ralph Bower; and his daughter, Catharine Royle, lived near its tip: but her house was much smaller than the Grove, and its garden lay separate, at the corner of Hawthorn Lane.

Next on the east side, opposite the Grove Inn, came two cottages occupied by bricklayers, and a house leased by a woman glazier, Mary Blower. She also leased four cottages on the other side of the island, on Green Lane, one of them occupied by a cotton weaver and the other by an ostler. In between these two groups of houses was a Methodist chapel, built about 1811, with a Sunday school of three hundred children. Later it was taken over by Congregationalists, so successfully that they started a new church and Sunday school in Chapel Lane in 1846.

The old chapel then became a library and reading room, and, in 1879, the British Workman hall and café, successor to the temperance public house which the Manchester City Mission, impressed by the number of drunken waggon drivers setting out from Wilmslow, had opened in 1874 in Bank Square on the site of the present Midland Bank and inscribed 'A Public House, without the drink, Where men may meet, read, talk, and think': attendance was so great that the larger premises in Grove Street were acquired. The new café, on the site of the bricklayers'

cottages, and seen here projecting with a bracket lamp into the pavement on the right, was equipped with benches like a tap room, and provided with newspapers and periodicals, until the second world war. By then it was the Cosy Café; in 1957, along with the hall behind, it was sold to Tesco's.

The shop the man has just passed marks the site of Wilmslow's old post office. In the 1840s the postmaster was Dr. Joseph Dean, who reputedly frequently walked to Manchester and back after an early tea, and who, with the help of his family, delivered the post as far away as Styal, Chorley, and Dean Row. Next door to him was the blacksmith, James Henshaw, who himself had eight children, and next door again, Francis Poole, grocer, said to have had the first shop in Grove Street. At their back, on Green Lane, were a garden and three cottages, the most prominent occupant being James Barker, the carrier to Stockport.

In 1841 only ten families lived in Grove Street, eight of them on the east side. Ten years later there were still only three on the west side, but the number on the east side had doubled to sixteen: they were a farmer, a schoolmaster, a nail manufacturer, a dealer in cotton yarn cloth, the parish clerk, three land and house proprietors, two tailors, two grocers, a blacksmith, a shoemaker, a servant, and an agricultural labourer.

The blacksmith

In 1851 there were seventeen blacksmiths in Wilmslow, but only two of them were in the central area: James Henshaw (who came from Prestbury) in Mill Lane, and John Heathe (from Chelford) in Grove Street; ten years earlier there had been another one, John Barnshaw, in Manchester Road.

The smithy in Grove Street was towards the south end, in a group of buildings on the east side; next door was the post office, and, the other way, Francis Poole the grocer: otherwise this stretch of the street was undeveloped, and opposite there was only William Gratrex's house between the toll-bar and the Grove Inn. Then in 1858 Robert Bourne arrived in Grove Street to set up business as grocer and flour dealer, and in (or about) 1884 he built blocks of shops on both sides at the south end,

19. Looking north along Grove Street

the one on the east side including his own animal foodstuffs business and the blacksmiths' house.

By this time the smith was S. Lomas, a qualified veterinary surgeon, who had practised also in Water Lane and Swan Street. From his house in Grove Street his surgery, stables, and smithy stretched back to Green Lane. He died in 1919 and was succeeded by his son H. Lomas, M.R.C.V.S., who was also a local food inspector; on his death in 1936 the veterinary practice closed: but the smithy continued until the 1960s when the premises were demolished to make way for shops.

Lomas's last smith was Mr. George Mottershead, who was with him for forty-eight years. He began work on the fourth of August, 1914: his first job was sharpening bayonets (in the second world war Lomas's made anchors for R.A.F. rescue launches). His apprenticeship was a wandering one, embracing Ollerton and Salford; that way he could improve his experience and his income: when he was eighteen he was earning ten shillings a week with board. At the time of the first world war the cost of a set of shoes for a pony was 7/6, and for a large cart horse £1. Some horses wore out their shoes in a week, but others, like the council horse, were light on their feet and their shoes lasted three months. Farm horses often had their feet pared and their shoes—called 'removes'—put on again.

The rural air which lingered about Bourne's feeding stuffs shop in Grove Street thickened at the rear on Green Lane. Near the smithy was a saddler, and, next door, Hill's, wheelwright and coachbuilder, whose premises, like Lomas's, stretched through from one street to the other. When carts needed new iron tyres the wheels were taken down Green Lane to cottages where peat was stored: over a peat fire the rims were made red hot, put round the wheels, then doused in water to contract them. Turf was also stored over the fire station in Green Lane, where Mr. Lomas was lieutenant of the voluntary brigade; the horses used were at Bradley's cab yard in Swan Street, but in the event of a fire it might be necessary to stop cabs in the street and take their horses.

20. S. Lomas, veterinary surgeon and blacksmith, Green Lane, c.1908

Wilmslow's shops

The first reference to shops in Wilmslow is by Samuel Finney: speaking of the 1740s, he says trade was then confined to a few petty retailers who supplied 'treacle, brown sugar, salt, tobacco, coarse linens and woollens, and other small necessaries'. By 1785, however, as a result of increasing industrialisation, the number of shopkeepers had 'increased amazingly, some of whom dealt in a great variety of articles . . . tea, coffee, loafe sugar, spices, printed cottons, calicoes, lawns, fine linens, silks, velvets, silk waistcoat pieces, silk cloaks, hats, bonnets, shawls, laced caps and a variety of other things'. Because of a shortage of cash, Ralph Bower found it necessary to pay wages at intervals of a few hours so that money spent by the first group of workers could be recovered from the shopkeepers to pay the next group.

In the 1740s there were only two shoemakers, but about a dozen clogmakers who used leather from old shoes brought in from neighbouring towns. By 1785 the position had been reversed: there were now a dozen shoemakers and perhaps only two clogmakers. In 1851 footwear was the biggest retail trade in Wilmslow—a

21. Robert Bourne, grocer, corn merchant, and baker, Grove Street

22. Thomas Passant, grocer, Grove Street

24. Johnson, saddler and harness maker, Grove Street

23. Thomas Hopley, grocer, Church Street

25. Charles K. Bransby, chemist, Grove Street

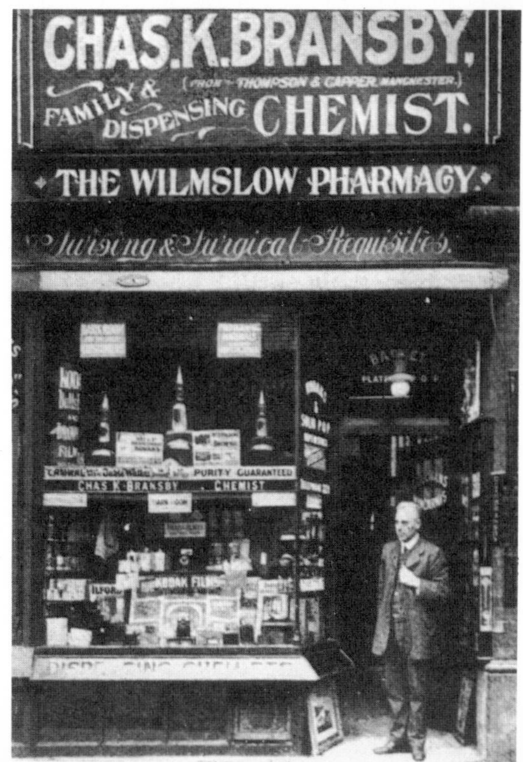

measure of the amount of walking in those days: thirty-nine shoemakers and four cloggers. Dressmakers came next with thirty-eight, then grocers with twenty-three.

In 1851 Church Street was the main shopping street in Wilmslow, with twenty-one of the thirty-six shops in the central streets: six grocers, four shoemakers, four tailors, two bakers, one butcher, one dressmaker, one hairdresser, one saddler, and one crumpet seller. Grove Street, on the other hand, was still mainly residential; out of nineteen houses perhaps five were shops: two grocers, two tailors, and a shoemaker.

A continuous tradition exists for some Wilmslow shops from the mid-nineteenth century. Thus in 1858 Robert Bourne arrived with a handcart from Bowdon and set up business in Grove Street as provision merchant, corn dealer, and pig-killer. He built several shops in Grove Street, as well as a number of houses in the street, which bears his name, next to the Friends' Meeting House. In 1868 Clement Owen came from Manchester in a 'horse drawn pantechnicon' and set up a wine shop in the house he had bought from William Gratrex, attorney and solicitor.

Mr. Warburton, in his eighties when he died in 1969, had been a grocer. He remembered how, before 1914, Wilmslow was a centre for outlying farm people who either walked in or came in their traps which they left behind his father's shop in Swan Street while they did their shopping; when they went home they took a big grocery order away with them. There was a great trade in corn, and especially oats, in those days, because of the horses. Mr. Warburton took over the business on the death of his father in 1910. When he came back from the first world war he got rid of all the old equipment in the shop, which had formerly done everything, including grind the corn and smoke the bacon.

The new road

Manchester Road was part of Wilmslow's first exercise in traffic modernisation—by accident. In the 1770s Samuel Finney wanted to include Wilmslow in the turnpike from Congleton to Manchester. Utilising the old road would mean widening Chancel Lane, either by eating into the churchyard on one side, which the parishioners would not tolerate, or by demolishing the houses on the other, which was too expensive for the turnpike commissioners. He found the solution in the construction of an entirely new road near the corn mill: 'all the difficulties were easily got over by my Lord Stamford's consent, and his Directions to two or three of his Tenants to supply the wants of the Commissioners. The Bridge was immediately Built, and the Road planned from the Hill Top without entering the Town of Wilmslow (except the South End of it). This proved a great mortification to the Town's People, who too late saw their Error, and in all probability will be of great future advantage to the Noble Earl's Estate, through whose Land, on both Sides, the New Road goes'.

To become a street a road needs houses. Manchester Road was cut in 1775, but it was only in 1787 that houses were begun: 'this year', says Finney, 'a beginning having been made in building in the New Road, by the Mill through Ladyfield, it is probable a new Street will rise up there in a few years'. What construction Finney is referring to is not known, but the date of the principal development in Manchester Road is certain: as Finney had foreseen, it took the form of a strip of plots, on the west side of the road, leased for building by the Earl of Stamford. From the evidence of surviving deeds, it seems probable that all the plots were leased simultaneously on 1 August 1792.

Thus, on that day, the Earl of Stamford leased a plot of $221\frac{1}{2}$ square yards to William Gibbon, tailor, bounded on the east by 'the new diverted Turnpike Road

26. The west side of Manchester Road, 1971

leading from Manchester through Wilmslow to Congleton', on the west by land belonging to John Trafford, on the north by another plot of land 'intended to be this day leased to John Worthington', and on the south by another plot 'intended to be this day leased to John Royle'. The lease was for three lives, and the yearly rent was £1 16 11. Before a year was out Gibbon was to erect at his own cost one or more houses three storeys high exclusive of cellars, with sashed windows, 'cornished to the front', and worth at least £5 per annum; certain noxious trades were banned: butcher, slaughter man, tallow chandler, soap maker, soap boiler, fellmonger, dyer.

Development on the east side of Manchester Road came only in the late nineteenth century: as late as 1872 there were houses only near the top of the hill at Warham Street, and at the bottom near Bollin Walk. In 1851 there were 174 people living in the road in forty houses. The street had a good social spread, divided fairly evenly between 'small' people—eleven cotton and silk workers, four journeyman craftsmen, three labourers—and 'considerable' people—six shopkeepers, one farmer, one innkeeper, one manufacturer, one merchant, two land or house proprietors, one doctor, two teachers. Among the independent people was John Bower, now aged seventy and a widower, the youngest son of the Ralph Bower who brought cotton mills to Wilmslow at the end of the eighteenth century. Significantly, his house was on the edge of the Bower domain, at the corner of Manchester Road and Mill Brow. Living with him in 1851 was his son, John, corndealer and draper, but his second son, Elijah, described as artist in 1841, was now a grocer in Grove Street. To them both, and to his married daughter, Elizabeth Daniel, he left, at his death in 1853, substantial properties in houses and land, and shares in the silk mill in the Carrs.

The railway

Wilmslow station was opened on 10 May 1842. It was on the Manchester and Birmingham Railway's line, which the company never got further than Crewe. While it was being cut in 1841 the railway added 543 to Wilmslow's population—'excavators' and their families, who put up in cottages and lodging houses, mostly in Chancel Lane, Church Street, Mill Street, and Mill Brow.

As originally constructed, the station had two platforms, with a goods yard on the west side. In 1894 the newly formed Urban District Council complained bitterly in an open letter to the *Wilmslow advertiser* about the disgraceful condition of the station and its failure to measure up to the status of the town. Opportunity to rebuild the station came with expansion of the railway: as suburban development spread south from Manchester and to the west of the existing railway the need was felt for a loop line from Longsight to Wilmslow via Styal. The new line was opened on 1 May 1909, and included, at Wilmslow, the provision of two additional platforms on the site of the old goods yard.

In 1850 Bagshaw's directory, speaking about Alderley Edge, noted that 'since the completion of the railway to this place, many elegant residences have been built,

27. Wilmslow railway station, before 1909

principally occupied by the merchants of Manchester, invited hither by the fine air, and the extensive and interesting views of the surrounding country. The first house was built here in 1845, since which about thirty very handsome residences have been erected'. However, the businessmen from Manchester were invited to Wilmslow and Alderley Edge not only by elegant residences but also by free railway tickets: in order, presumably, to establish a captive travelling public along its newly constructed line, the railway company offered free season tickets for twenty one years to those who built a house worth at least £50 a year within one mile of Wilmslow or Alderley Edge stations. It is a sad postscript to an ingenious idea that today Wilmslow has the largest proportion of car-commuting businessmen in the country.

LONDON & NORTH WESTERN RAILWAY.
MANCHESTER & BIRMINGHAM SECTION. No. 2
Mr Benjn Gibbons
having erected a Dwelling house of the annual Value of at least fifty pounds within one Mile from the Alderley Station is entitled for a term of twenty one years commencing from the sixth day of October 1846 a
FREE PASS OVER THE RAILWAY TO AND FROM ALDERLEY AND MANCHESTER
By Order
Secretary of the Manchester & Birmingham Committee

28. Railway pass, Alderley to Manchester, 1846

The old road

The first photograph shows four old houses at the corner of Water Lane and Hawthorn Street. They appear in the 25″ O.S. plan of 1872; in the 1898 25″ O.S. plan they have been reduced to three by the loss of the southernmost house; and in the 1909 25″ O.S. plan they have been completely replaced by the row of new houses which appears in the second illustration.

These old houses raise some interesting questions about the ancient route through Wilmslow from the south. In a suggestive but (to use his favourite word) somewhat sinuous discussion of the road between Alderley and Wilmslow in *Cheshire notes and queries*, 1896, a very knowledgeable local inhabitant whose memory reaches back to the 1830s, and who writes under the pseudonym of Cedric, debates which sections of the road are ancient and which date from the construction of the turnpike in the late 18th century. In particular, he considers, in ample but elusive detail, the route between Fulshaw cross and Parsonage Green.

He decides, from the absence of old houses and the name of the New Inn, that this last stretch of the Alderley road dates almost wholly from the turnpike. 'Hold hard. Then where did the old road go?'. At Fulshaw cross a corner of the vast Lindow Common came right up to the Knutsford road. The King's Arms (built, Cedric thinks, about 1830) stood on a triangle of land enclosed from the Common in comparatively modern times. Opposite the inn, and immediately to the north, was the 'wild heath', used for pigeon shooting and suchlike games, and a black lake, used for skating in winter time. From Fulshaw cross to the bottom of Hawthorn Street (where Bedells Lane now runs) was nothing but an almost impassable 'sludgy track'.

As far as the end of Chapel Lane the road from Fulshaw cross followed, Cedric suggests, its present route. But from then on to Parsonage Green the ground was open common, so the 'highway wriggled along as best it could upon the soundest parts', linking together a number of old houses, now mostly gone but which Cedric could remember, in the area between Hawthorn Street and the present Alderley Road. He points in particular to 'several very ancient houses, notably one where Joshua Sumner lived, and also one in Mr. Dale's field on the eastern side [of Hawthorn Street]. This old cottage was inhabited for many years by old Sarah

29. The corner of Water Lane and Hawthorn Street, before 1898

Thompson, and it had several very venerable trees growing about it, showing it to be on a highway'. As it approached the present Water Lane Cedric's route skirted 'close by (on the southern side) the Old Inn or hostelry'. This was probably one of the houses illustrated here, called the Old Inn to distinguish it from its successor on the new turnpike. Cedric describes the Old Inn as 'now owned by Mrs. Clulow', and says 'a portion, evidently an added portion' fell down 'last year' (which fits in very

30. The corner of Water Lane and Hawthorn Street, c.1900

well with the reduced size of the row shown in the 1898 25″ O.S. plan). For him it was 'an ancient building, but not one of the most ancient; and yet reeds were used in it instead of laths'. But on the opposite side of his 'supposed road there was fifty years ago, and less, an old framed house, now demolished, on land now belonging to Mr. Moses Broughton . . . [with] a noble row of pines growing along this route, indicating a place of importance'. Finally, still wriggling about over 'the then open Common (for Water-lane is too straight and too modern in its present form to be considered)' Cedric's ancient road found its way to Parsonage Green.

Consonant with the way in which, in general, the road into Wilmslow from the south is seen in Burdett's map of 1777 to hug the side of the great Common, Cedric is no doubt right in suggesting that, in detail, it must have hopped about among the boggy outcrops of moss which were scattered as far as Parsonage Green; and no doubt he is right, too, in feeling that its route is to be associated with old houses. Some mysteries, however, remain.

Firstly, Cedric's route inclines surprisingly far to the west. Would it not have been possible to find a more direct route to Parsonage Green—to the east, if need be, of the present Alderley Road? Even allowing for the difficulties of terrain Cedric's road has a painfully dog's hind leg angularity about it. Secondly, it is interesting that Cedric, while looking for an oblique approach, should dismiss the claim of Hawthorn Street, which has the palpable feel of an ancient way. Hawthorn Street was formerly called Pepper Street, and Cedric gives it another early name—Lindow Side, 'which it really was'. Certainly it was the first practicable south-north route on the east side of the Common, but Cedric thinks most of the houses in Hawthorn Street 'not very ancient', and prefers the route which he strings between his ancient houses to the east. Further, Hawthorn Street has the look of aiming straight at Hawthorn Hall, a site more ancient than any we can be certain about for Wilmslow village itself. One would have expected a route to Hawthorn Hall to determine also the approach to the centre of Wilmslow. Is it possible, in fact, that this route to Hawthorn Hall was continued by a road on the other side of the present Hawthorn Lane, a road which has now disappeared but which aimed at Bollin Hall and the original nucleus of Wilmslow—William's hill—merging on the way with the connection which Cedric elsewhere suggests Hawthorn Hall had with the village?

If the most meaningful objective of either Cedric's reconstructed route or Hawthorn Street was the old Wilmslow centre by the river, what route would best serve Parsonage Green, a separate hamlet in early times? Is it possible that the way from Fulshaw cross followed, in fact, however tentatively, something like the route of the present road? Such a road is indeed dotted in on a Trafford estate map of 1771. Of course, it may be an indication of the turnpike to come; but, then, Cedric's route is omitted altogether.

III · The Bollin Valley

Wilmslow's bridges

We are less aware of local bridges than our ancestors were: we need notices to tell us which rivers we are crossing. Anciently, maintenance of bridges was imposed on their subjects by Anglo-Saxon kings; in later days it became a county responsibility. Wilmslow has moved away from the Bollin, but when its centre of gravity lay nearer the river, the bridges that crossed it were a matter of general interest.

When Samuel Finney returned from London to Wilmslow and busied himself in local affairs, roads and bridges were among his principal concerns:

> 'It was very remarkable that almost all the Country Bridges in the Hundred of Macclesfield were about this time so much fallen to decay, that they were obliged to be repaired and widened or rebuilt; few of them were above Ten feet wide, the Facing Stones not above nine Inches thick, and the Foundations generally faulty, particularly in the Wing Walls. It was supposed most of the Bridges had been built about the same time (about one hundred years before), as they were of the same construction. All those upon the River Bolin and Deanwater, in the neighbourhood of Wimslow, were referred by the Quarter Sessions to the immediate care of Mr. Wright [of Mottram Hall] and Mr. Finney'.

The first bridge repaired by this busy couple was Oversleyford; next came Handforth, which was very expensive—about £500—because of the new turnpike road; then Deanwater, which cost £80.

Wilmslow presented problems similar to those of Handforth. A turnpike had been constructed from Congleton to Wilmslow. To the north, beyond Handforth, lay the turnpike to Manchester. To unite the two it was necessary to improve the way out of Wilmslow, which ran down Church Street, over the bridge by the Church (built in 1771 by public subscription), then through Lacey Green and Stanneylands. Finney proposed a widening of Chancel Lane by cutting into the churchyard and raising the roadway about three feet, 'which would have gained an easy Passage both for Waggons and Coaches'; but when he explained his ideas at a vestry meeting 'such was the Superstitious Bigotry, and Folly of the People, that he was almost hooted out of the Town with his Profane Proposals'. However, after consultation with the engineer of the turnpike trust Finney lighted on a passage of the Bollin near the corn mill, passing through land belonging to Lord Stamford. 'The Bridge was immediately Built, and the Road planned from the Hill Top without entering the Town of Wilmslow (except the South End of it)'.

The last bridge Wright and Finney tackled was Vardon, by which the road to Stockport crossed the Bollin. Like the others, it was 'much too narrow and fallen to decay', though it had been repaired a few years before. So they decided to pull it down altogether and build a new one; also to make a new, straighter road, 'and raise it greatly through the Valley, in order to make the ascent easy on both sides'. The builder was Anderson from Yorkshire, 'who had already given elegant specimens of his Genius in the two Bridges of Cheadle and Congleton'. Altogether, the bridge (illustrated here) and the road cost the county over £800, 'and gave the Gentlemen who had the care of it such a Surfeit of Bridge Building that no consideration will ever after induce them to undertake another. This great work took up the space of two years before it was completed in 1786'.

31. Vardon bridge

Wilmslow's weir

The broad waters of the weir hang like skeins of white wool between the stout stone abutments. From the centre of the bank above juts the sluice gate which feeds water into the narrow mill lade. Skeletons of trees stand mutely in the mysterious valley. Victorian castles—The Towers, Fawns Keep, Stokes Lacey—look down from their northern escarpment; a snug, cast-iron, trellis-work bridge crosses the river to Wilmslow Park. Meanwhile the original manor house has become a builder's yard, and the ancient park of the Fittons, the Venables, and the Booths stretches unnoticed to where an embankment and a ragged row of trees carries the parish boundary north from the Bollin and east of Dean Row.

32. Bollin weir

In 1246 Richard Fitton had a mill, worth six marks a year. No doubt it was near his hall, but its precise site is unknown. The medieval wheel would be undershot, placed directly into the river. The present mill site is away from the river, so either the medieval mill was on a different site (though some evidence of an earlier building still exists in the foundations of the present building) or the river must have changed its course (which it readily does on the wide, flat floor of the Bollin valley).

Nothing further is known of the history of Wilmslow corn mill until modern times. Curiously, Burdett's map of Cheshire of 1777, which indicates water mills, does not show the existence of one at Wilmslow. The date of the construction of the weir and the mill lade is unknown—perhaps early nineteenth century like the present mill building?

The silk mill

A little girl in a cloche hat dunks her stone in the still water; the ripples she makes are the only movement in a scene immobilised, yet heavy with change. Across the river are the ruins of Wilmslow's silk mill. All that remains today is a faint line of stones across the bed of the river, and a few bricks in the bank on the other side. The building is in ruins because it was burnt down in 1923 when it was storing gelatine. Before that it was a laundry, before that a silk mill, and before that, perhaps, one of several small cotton mills which arose in Wilmslow at the end of the eighteenth and the beginning of the nineteenth century. William Norbury confidently identifies it with the first of these cotton mills, built by Ralph Bower in the 1780s, but there is little doubt that this stood higher up the Bollin alongside the church. The silk mill became known as Barber's mill in the nineteenth century, but Norbury is correct in saying that it was not built by Charles Barber: the will of John Bower of 1853 makes it clear that the mill was merely rented by Barber from the Bowers.

The millkeeper's house which the illustration shows intact has now also gone; but besides the few sticks and stones there remain two other evidences of the site of the mill. One is the spasmodic line of trees southward across the Carrs, marking the boundary between the Hawthorn and Pownall estates, and pointing directly from the silk mill to Hawthorn Hall, principal home of the Bowers from about 1800; the other, the magnificent avenue of beech trees, traditionally known as Silk Lane, which led to the mill from the foot of Cliff Road.

Unlike the corn mill, the silk mill did not have a lade—simply a small weir which, with the force of the river at this narrow point, was sufficient to drive an undershot wheel.

33. The silk mill

The laundry

The old silk mill burnt down on 4 October 1923. By then it was reportedly storing gelatine, cellophane, or (less likely) gelignite. Immediately before that it had been Bray's Sanitary Laundry: 'situated in the heart of this pretty country district . . . pure air, perfect cleanliness . . . we return everything but the dirt . . . our motive power is WATER, so we make no smuts to fall on your linen whilst generating steam'. Cotton chemises cost from 1½d, drawers and flannel petticoats from 2d, wool or union combinations from 3d, dressing jackets from 4d, and linen cuffs from 1d a pair.

Lit by electricity, the laundry had 'the most perfect machine for imparting a good finish to Table Damasks'. There were also a shirt finishing machine, a collar machine, a goffering machine, and a machine for erecting shirt collar bands; gas irons were used for 'bodying shirts and for ironing under and fancy clothing': in the washhouse were a washing machine and a hydro-extractor. The Sorting and Packing Goods department was supervised by the manageress, and every care was taken to 'prevent mistakes, this desirable end being greatly facilitated when customers' goods are plainly marked with name'.

34. The laundry (a)

35. The laundry (b)

36. The laundry (c)

Pownall bridge

The way across Pownall bridge is now thought of as a pleasant entrance to the Carrs, or a bridle path which motorists would like to use as much as horses. But as late as, certainly, 1831 it was the main route to Pownall Hall: neither the ceremonial avenue from Altrincham Road nor the extension of Hawthorn Lane to give access to Pownall Hall appear on a map until 1842.

Originally there was simply a ford across the river, but when Quarry Bank mill raised its weir about 1800 T.J. Worrall of Pownall Hall complained that his ford had become impassable. Greg, therefore, agreed to erect a wooden bridge if Worrall provided the timber, but when this was swept away in 1820 by the force of the river, Greg contributed £40 and materials, and Worrall £20, to the building of a brick bridge.

The neighbourhood of this crossing of the Bollin once had a significance which has now disappeared. About half a mile away to the north, somewhere on the high ground overlooking the right bank of the Dean, was Norcliffe Hall, a medieval predecessor of the Norcliffe Hall built by R.H. Greg in Styal about 1830. Dependent on it was a manor which existed separately from the Bollin estate from the mid-thirteenth century till 1598; the two manors were then reunited and known as Bollin-cum-Norcliffe.

Also somewhere nearby was a mill. We know precisely when it was erected—1335—from a grant made by John Fitton to his son Richard of a piece of land in Morley on which to build it; the inhabitants of Morley were released from using Bollin mill presumably on condition of using the new one. Earwaker knew of its remains, 'in what is at present a large willow-bed, not far from the junction of the two rivers, the Bollin and the Dean, at Twinney Bridge'. These remains seem now to have disappeared, but the site of the mill is suggested by the names of two fields, Higher and Lower Mill Field, on the opposite side of the Bollin.

Quarry Bank Mill

After the woods, the sudden, untenanted bulk of Quarry Bank Mill stretches, warmly glowing like an abandoned Cistercian monastery, along the green valley bottom, a vacant memorial to the rural phase of the industrial revolution. The invention of

37. Pownall bridge

Hargreaves' spinning jenny and Arkwright's frame brought a rush for water power to the banks of suitable streams. The little cotton mills in Wilmslow have long gone, but the success of smaller men in tapping the water of the Bollin, and creating a labour supply for spinning, led Samuel Greg, a rich Manchester cotton manufacturer, after exploring Lancashire and Derbyshire, to choose Quarry Bank for a much larger mill where he could card, slub, and spin cotton yarn for warp.

Greg leased land from Lord Stamford in January 1784. By early summer the mill was in operation: the first employee, a local girl, Peggy Chapman, started work in May. It was a four-storey building, ninety feet long by thirty feet wide, with mullioned windows and a little bell tower. There were three thousand spindles, worked by two wooden water wheels of ten feet diameter. The total cost, including machinery, was £16,000. Brazilian cotton was used, costing five shillings a pound; after spinning into warp for the finest muslins it sold at twenty shillings a pound. The men earned from ten to twelve shillings a week, the women five shillings, and the children from one-and-sixpence to two shillings. Each day two drays set out with the manufactured yarn for the Bridgewater canal at Broadheath where Greg had a warehouse, and returned with raw cotton which had come by barge from Liverpool. This system lasted for nearly ninety years.

The mill prospered for forty years; lost £15,000 between 1825 and 1840; thought, nevertheless, of buying the whole of Styal and part of Morley in 1828; introduced powerloom weaving in 1835; stopped spinning in 1896; and closed altogether on Friday, 30 October 1959 when the last three women workers were making dish-cloths and laundry bags. Today, along with the remarkable Greg estate of workers' houses, chapel, school, and farms, Quarry Bank Mill belongs to the National Trust.

38. Quarry Bank Mill, 1960

Samuel Greg, 1756–1834

Samuel Greg's father was a Belfast ship-owner. His ancestors were Scottish, but a grandfather had established himself as a merchant in Belfast in 1714. His mother, Elizabeth Hyde, came from Ardwick. After education at Harrow, Greg rejected the idea of the Presbyterian ministry and accepted instead an invitation from his uncles, Robert and Nathaniel, to join their business of check and fustian manufacturers in Manchester. After a grand tour of Europe he became aware of the new inventions in the cotton industry and began to search for a site for a cotton mill.

Greg's first lease of the site at Quarry Bank was taken out in 1784. Initially, he continued to deal also with his uncle's business in Manchester, but when his partner, Massey, died shortly after the mill opened, Greg moved to Styal with his new wife,

39. Samuel Greg

Hanna (Lightbody) in 1787; his children, however, were born in the house (still surviving) which he retained in King Street. Soon after coming to Styal he had built, close to the mill, a new residence, Quarry Bank House, which he quickly extended and surrounded with ample gardens.

'The house', said John Morley, 'over which this excellent woman [Mrs. Greg] presided, offered an ideal picture of domestic felicity, with the grave simplicity of the household, their intellectual ways, the absence of display and even of knick-knacks, the plain blue walls, the comfortable furniture, the well filled bookcases, the portrait of George Washington over the chimney piece'.

And Catherine Stanley wrote, 'Have you ever been to Quarry Bank? It is such a picture of rational happy life. Mr. Greg is quite a gentleman; his daughters have the delightful simplicity of people who are perfectly satisfied in their place and never trying to get out of it. He is rich, and he spends, just as rich people do not generally spend their money, keeping a sort of open house without pretension. If he has more guests than the old butler can manage he has his maid-servants in to wait. He seldom goes out except on journeys, so that with the almost certainty of finding a family party at home, a large circle of connections, and literary people, and foreigners, and scotch and irish, are constantly dropping in, knowing they cannot come amiss. You may imagine how this sort of life makes the whole family sit loose to all the incumbrances and hindrances of society. They actually do not know what it is to be formal or dull; each with their separate pursuits and tasks, intelligent and well informed'.

Quarry Bank Mill: the water power

Little is certain about Styal before the Gregs: they moved roads, the cross, the village green, even the name Quarry Bank. As a result, the earlier history of the place has a legendary air: recluses (a hermit called Disley, then a family called Murrall) living in a cave, known as the Kirk, in the river bank; salters using the cave as a camp on their route to the wiches; Jersey woolmen from Yorkshire beating a trail with pack-horses across the Bollin. However, the Gregs put the caves to more mundane uses:

the one on the left in the illustration, as a boathouse; the Kirk (on the right) to house sluice machinery for the dam.

Water supply was one of three factors which led Samuel Greg to choose Quarry Bank as the site for his mill (the other two were transport facilities and labour supply). From Pownall ford there was a fourteen foot fall in the river, sufficient to turn the mill's two first wooden wheels. In 1795 Peter Ewart, a Scottish engineer trained by Boulton and Watt, became a partner of Greg, and made extensive alterations. The mill was doubled in length, a fifth storey was added, a fresh weir was built to give a greater head of water, and the original wooden wheels were replaced by an enormous iron one—32′ in diameter, 21′ wide, weighing 43 tons, and producing 100 nominal horse-power. About 1800 the weir was raised again, creating a mill pool of five acres, but involving Greg in difficulties with neighbouring landowners: he had to buy land from Trafford to take the overspill, and build a bridge for Worrall to replace Pownall ford.

Then between 1817 and 1819, to increase power once more, Greg built a tunnel beneath the woods between the mill and the river three-quarters of a mile away. No engineer was called in: Greg superintended the work himself. The tunnel was cut mainly through rock—with pick and shovel and an immense quantity of gunpowder. Everyone was employed, including the apprentices, who worked overtime. One man was killed by falling stone in the wheelrace. The tunnel cost £5,000, and a new water wheel, weighing 36 tons, £2,300. Altogether, between 1818 and 1820, on this work and on an extension to the mill, Greg spent £17,564. These were the last big alterations to Quarry Bank Mill, although yet another wheel was installed in 1847, to be superseded by water driven turbines in 1904.

40. Quarry Bank Mill dam, 1960

The 'Prentice House

The apprentices' house of Quarry Bank Mill was built about 1790, to house a hundred boys and girls between the ages of nine and twenty-one. The best first-hand information about the house comes from evidence given by two boys, Joseph Fulton (seventeen) and Thomas Priestly (thirteen), when they were brought before the Middlesex magistrates in 1806, having 'eloped and deserted the service of Samuel Greg'; they had walked all the way from Styal to London to see their families and been arrested four weeks later.

They said they were satisfied with the treatment they received at Styal, and went on to describe it in detail. There were forty-two boy and more girl apprentices. They lodged in the 'Prentice House near the mill and were under the care of Richard Sims and his wife. The boys slept at one side of the house, the girls at the other. The rooms were very clean, and aired every day; the floors were frequently washed, and the walls were whitewashed once a year. 'Our beds were good. We slept two in a bed and had clean sheets once a month. We had clean shirts every Sunday and new clothes for Sunday once in two years; also new working jackets when those in use were worn out . . . On Sunday we went to Church in the morning and to school in the afternoon, after which we had time to play'.

The information given about the apprentices by Alfred Fryer, who was friendly with Robert Hyde Greg, is even fuller, but it was gathered a generation after the apprenticeship system came to an end. On the whole it confirms the evidence of the two boys, but the hard truth which shone through their naked candour is now smooth with special pleading.

'The young people were required to rise betimes in the morning ready to attend at the mill at half-past five, after consuming a piece of good wholesome, but not quite white bread. At half-past eight breakfast was served, and as only ten minutes were allowed for that meal it was taken in the mill. Oatmeal porridge with abundance of skimmed milk, if not too hot, can be placed out of sight in a remarkably short time. The dinner hour—which, by the way, was only half an hour in duration—commenced at one o'clock. The dinner, like the other meals, was abundant in quantity and simple and wholesome in quality. Potatoes and bacon was the usual

41. The Apprentice House, 1960

repast; sometimes a ham was substituted, and more rarely butcher's meat. Those who preferred buttermilk to bacon were allowed to have it. Sometimes the dinner consisted of hot stew. On Sunday cold boiled ham, home cured and appetising, was usually seen, and in spring and summer, raised fruit pies of rhubarb or gooseberry sometimes made an agreeable variety. 'Barm dumplings', too, occasionally made their appearance. The afternoon meal was served at half-past five, and consisted of oatmeal porridge and skimmed milk. It was partaken of pretty much as the Israelites partook of the feast of the Passover. The long day's work was terminated at half-past eight, and a piece of bread served for supper. An exception was made on Friday, for the supper on that evening consisted of broth. . . . Sunday was a happy day, and served to break the monotony of the week. After dinner the school was held, and

42. Quarry Bank Mill workers, before 1896

then all the Misses Greg came up from Quarry Bank and taught the young people. Instruction was given in reading, writing, and arithmetic; and whilst paper and pens were employed by the more advanced scholars, the younger ones (in those days of quill pens and paper duty) commenced their education by tracing figures on a sanded board'.

Spinners, weavers, wheelwrights

Fourteen dignified men, twelve of them bearded like the pard, dress for the past in fustian waistcoats, cotton jackets, mufflers, and a rich assortment of headgear which includes tartan-check and Lenin-style glazed peak caps, deerstalkers, and an Alice-in-Wonderland carpenter's paper square; but the future's fascinated gaze they return with skilled and easy solidarity. Set before the Gregs' private coach-house doors, with upraised hammer and clenched spanners, very likely they are celebrating the fitting of new segments into the great Quarry Bank Mill wheel, a wheelwright job they have all been helping with even though most of them are spinners and weavers.

The presence of spinners helps to date the photograph at a little before 1896 (when spinning stopped at Quarry Bank). In 1973 Mr. Samuel Henshall, 84, the last manager of Quarry Bank Mill, who started work there in 1901, could name all the group but one—a recently arrived 'stranger'. They were, from left to right, standing: James 'Puppy' Henshall (winding and warping overlooker), the stranger (weaving overlooker), John Hampson, John Moss (spinner), William Foden, James Wood (spinner), Henry Venables (in charge of the wheel), James Henshall, Tom Venables; sitting: John Burgess, William Travis (spinner), John Thompson (overlooker), James Moore, John Hopley.

IV · Historic houses

Preston Cottage

Many probate inventories—lists of the belongings of individuals made soon after their death—survive for houses in Wilmslow, but so far only one has been matched with a house which still stands: Preston Cottage, now in Alderley Edge but formerly in the Chorley township of Wilmslow.

Brook Lane was originally called Preston Lane, after a family of Prestons who lived in the house until 1590. In the early seventeenth century the house was occupied by a family called Dickens, and the inventory which survives was made in 1628 on the death of Edmund Dickens. It is the record of the goods and chattels, worth £224 17 11, of a substantial yeoman, who worked land in nine different places and kept his farming equipment at two houses. The inventory suggests that his house was a building of eight rooms: dwelling house, parlour, new parlour, buttery, old buttery, chamber over the buttery, corn chamber, and cellar (i.e. larder).

The early seventeenth century was a period of extensive rebuilding in England, either in the form of new houses or the enlargement of old ones. As houses grew in size the uses of their rooms changed. We can see this development taking place at Preston Cottage. In 1628 the house had been fairly recently extended by the addition of a new parlour and a new buttery. The 'dwelling house' (that is, the main room of the house, in the southern half of England called the hall) was still very much the central, multi-purpose room, combining living room, work room, dining room, kitchen, and store room for small agricultural equipment; but sleeping had moved out—partly into the new parlour (one bed) and the old buttery (one bed), but mainly upstairs, into the chamber over the buttery (four beds) and the corn chamber (one bed).

The present structure of Preston Cottage ties in well with the inventory. Thus there is a substantial stone wall separating the main downstairs rooms from the next room, indicating that this was once the end of the house, and that the added room is the 'new parlour' of the inventory. The inventory does not mention a chamber over the new parlour, implying that this room was at first open to the roof; such a room is often referred to in other inventories as the 'great parlour', and the feature is confirmed in the case of Preston Cottage by the fact that the flooring for an upstairs room has clearly been inserted at a later date, involving the construction of a special staircase in the corner, the only means of access to this upstairs room.

Upstairs rooms were often used for storage as well as for sleeping. This is demonstrated by the Preston Cottage inventory in which the corn chamber is said to contain corn, oats, and kitchen equipment, as well as a bed. It is satisfying to learn, therefore, that when Mr. and Mrs. A.M. Flanagan began their sympathetic restoration of the house in 1968 they found fistsful of corn in the roof timbers and on the floor of the room over the middle of the house.

43. Preston Cottage, Brook Lane, Alderley Edge

Chorley Hall

As though in evocation of the peasants' clearing which gave the locality its Anglo-Saxon name, a touch of mist, bare trees, a half-filled moat, a deserted winter landscape, surround a lonely Chorley Hall.

At the front the building is jaunty with a magpie, half-timbered Tudor addition, but the rear is sombre with the stonework of an early fourteenth century house. Though the mullioned and transomed windows are seventeenth century insertions, still evident is the arched doorway of the medieval screens passage which separated hall from buttery, pantry, and kitchen. The hall was once a tall, spacious room, open to the roof, heated by a central hearth; and over the service rooms was the solar, also open to its timbered roof, and probably reached by an external staircase.

When the Davenports added the detached half-timbered building at the front in the mid-sixteenth century they also made major alterations to the old house: replaced the open hearth with a stone fireplace, raised the roof so as to insert new bedrooms over the hall, put in a winding staircase by the fireplace to reach these new rooms and the solar, and added a matching gable at the north end of the house.

There have been other alterations, improvements, restorations; but the building's architectural character and fine setting have survived. And today the moat is satisfyingly full: this feature of many quite small manor houses in the Wilmslow area—dictated more by mundane thoughts of drainage and abstract considerations of prestige than by serious purposes of military defence—has now gone from White Hall, Saltersley, and Hollingee. Only the magnificent example at Chorley remains.

Handforth Hall

Over the doorway of Handforth Hall is carved: 'this hall was builded in the year of our lord 1562 by Uryan Brereton knight'. A branch of the Breretons of Malpas acquired Handforth about 1530 when Sir Urian Brereton married Margaret Stanley (née Hondford), heiress of the medieval lords of Handforth. There must have been a medieval hall at Handforth, but no tradition of it survives. However, the present house is sufficient puzzle in itself.

At the end of his account of the hall Earwaker abruptly interjects, '. . . but no trace of there having been any quadrangle, and it is extremely improbable that any ever existed'. This apparently inconsequential remark was presumably prompted by Ormerod's contention that 'only one side of the quadrangle is standing'. That Ormerod was, in fact, right, and Earwaker wrong, is demonstrated by the probate

44. Chorley Hall

inventory which survives of William Brereton (nephew of the builder of the hall, and father of Sir William Brereton the parliamentary general) made after his death in 1610. The inventory shows that Handforth Hall at that time contained more than forty rooms, including a hall, armoury, knight's chamber, two 'houses of office', a 'sommer chamber', a gentlewomen's chamber, a schoolmaster's chamber, a nursery, and a chapel. Even more significantly, it had a gatehouse of at least four rooms, as well as barns, stables, and other outhouses.

The picture presented by the inventory is thus of a very substantial house indeed, much bigger than the present building, and perhaps the largest house in the Wilmslow neighbourhood. Moreover, it clearly had a courtyard with a gatehouse and farm buildings round it—a traditional medieval layout; it is interesting that such a style was still being adopted in 1562. With the death in 1674 of Sir Thomas Brereton, the last in the direct male line, the house went into decline. Shortly before or after his death it was sold to Thomas Legh of Adlington. In 1716 the Leghs sold it to William Wright of Mottram St. Andrew, and after that it passed through various hands. At some stage it must have been drastically reduced in size.

The puzzle remains as to where the courtyard was. At first the lie of Hall Lane suggests it would be on the north side, but this puts the porch on the outside of the quadrilateral, and makes the present building a remnant of the gatehouse, which it cannot be. Then one is reminded of the similarity of this porch to that at Adlington, where it leads into the screens passage of the great hall. An inscription over the Adlington porch says that this part of the house was built in 1581 by Thomas Legh who married Sybil, daughter of Sir Urian Brereton of Handforth. It seems likely, then, that the porch, and perhaps the quadrangle, at Adlington were modelled on those at Handforth. If so, the courtyard of Handforth Hall must have embraced an area now partly covered by the front garden of the present house.

45. Handforth Hall

Hawthorn Hall

Keyworth's pleasing pastoral reminds us that Hawthorn Hall was once surrounded by cows rather than houses. There is no doubt that the site is one of the ancient spots in Wilmslow: some sort of settlement was there at least as early as the thirteenth century, when the 'foundation' charter of the Wilmslow area refers to it as 'Harethorn'. There must, too, have been a medieval estate and hall, occupied by a branch of the Pownall family, but nothing is known about them. However, it is pretty clear that Hawthorn Street, an ancient route into Wilmslow from the south, made straight for the hall.

We do know something about the hall which preceded the present one. In 1606 the Pownalls sold the estate to John Latham of Irlam. Latham died in 1622, and an inventory was made of his house at Hawthorn. We can be certain that this house

46. Hawthorn Hall, c.1889

was not the medieval one from William Webb's description of it about 1621 as a 'fine new house built by John Lathum'. It must, therefore, have lasted less than a century.

Like most other houses of any size at this time, the seventeenth century Hawthorn Hall was a farm as well as a place to live in: John Latham, in fact, had twenty-five cows, seven horses, forty-six sheep, ten pigs, thirty hens, four turkeys, seven geese, and two ducks; some of his land was plainly arable because four of the horses were draught animals, and he had three harrows and two ploughs. But it was also a house of some pretension: there were four upstairs rooms as well as a maid's closet; downstairs there were a hall, parlour, buttery, dairyhouse, brewhouse, and kitchen, and outhouses including a garner and servants' stable. The parlour was remarkable in being a purely entertaining room, with tables, forms, chairs, cupboards, and carpets (i.e. table-cloths). Parlours were usually slept in at this time, and Hawthorn is the first instance in Wilmslow in which no bed is mentioned in the parlour. The hall, too, is unusual in containing only prestige furniture: two tables and forms, a clock with a bell, three pikes, and one old halberd. Most halls at this time were still developing from their origin as the single all-purpose room of the house: it is only the occasional house in which, as at Hawthorn, the hall has thrown off every primitive use—sleeping, cooking, eating—to become the formal reception area that it is today.

The seventeenth century Hawthorn Hall was thus not a very large house: nine rooms compared with more than forty in the contemporary Handforth Hall. But it was an example of the complete replacement of a medieval house, rather than its adaptation, during the housing revolution of the late sixteenth and early seventeenth century. And the novelty of a new house was matched by the modernness in the uses of its rooms.

Since the seventeenth century the Hawthorn estate has suffered frequent changes of ownership. In 1698 John Leigh, who had bought the estate about three years earlier from the Lathams, built the house which we know today. He died in 1720 and in his will spoke of the 'great charges' he had been put to in 'building, raising, and

furnishing' the house, with its 'summer houses, dove houses, barnes, stables . . . gardens, orchards, walks, fruit trees, fish ponds'. He left his estate to the younger sons of the Earl of Warrington, but to 'my cozen Elizabeth Dixon, in consideration of her having faithfully served me in the place of a Housekeeper for many years' he left all his 'Physicall Gally Potts and Glasses, Cordiall waters, Electuarys, Syrrupes, Ointments, Oiles, Plaisters, and all the Physick and Druggs, with the chest in which they came down from London', and all his 'Muffes, Shirts, and wareing Linnen and flannell, Cravatts, Ruffles, Neckcloathes of all sorts, and all my wareing swords and cloakes, with all my woollen cloathes, stockens, shooes, boots, spurs, and hats of all kinds whatsoever'.

After no less than five transfers of possession in the eighteenth century the house and the estate were acquired about 1800 by a very different kind of owner—Ralph Bower, yeoman farmer turned cotton spinner from Chorley, and harbinger of the industrial revolution in Wilmslow. When he bought it the estate must have retained some of its medieval extent: to the west it bordered the Pownall estate; to the north it ran down to the Bollin; to the east it stretched to Church Street; and to the south it reached as far as Parsonage Green. The Hall was linked with the village by a road variously described as a long drive starting from the neighbourhood of the parish church and, more confusingly, as 'a church road [through Dungeon Fold], which had steps down on each side of a dell with a rivulet at the bottom, which emerged in Church-street'.

After Ralph Bower's death in 1801 the Hawthorn estate was divided among his children, the Grove going to his eldest son William, and Hawthorn Hall to his third son Ralph. This Ralph died in 1834, leaving one son, William, who lived by the church and worked the cotton mill in Mill Lane, and a large family of daughters. For a short time the daughters and their widowed mother continued to live at the Hall. As a family they attended the Methodist chapel in Water Lane, and gave hospitality at the Hall to the itinerant Methodist ministers from Stockport. Once a year, in November, there was a missionary meeting at the chapel, 'into which great enthusiasm was thrown'. A temporary platform was built over the pews and filled

47. Forecourt of the Methodist chapel, Water Lane

'with no mean array of speakers', including Methodist preachers, laymen from the Church of England, 'and an array of what I might call Stockport squires, who were favourable to missions, and who had no objection to meeting a choice company at the old Hawthorn Hall'. For children it was a high day, a red letter day, with the everlasting report which no one wanted to hear, the great guns who were to make great speeches, the returned missionary who exhibited outlandish costumes and wooden idols, and the man or two who could introduce a little comedy. Then came retirement to the hospitable board at Hawthorn Hall, and lastly a ride, late at night, in a special coach.

Hawthorn Hall School

In 1835 Mrs. Bower and her daughters moved from Hawthorn Hall and their place was taken by a boarding school which Mr. Sutherland, a former Methodist missionary, had been running at Green Hall; he and his scholars attended Water Lane chapel, and the school became popular with wealthy Methodist families. Between the two occupations the house was possibly empty for a time because Andrew Pearson describes how, as a boy, he and other lads used to peep through the old white gates in Hawthorn Lane to get a glimpse of the ghosts who were reputed to haunt the Hall. 'There was a long row of tall poplars on the south side and numerous black firs on the other side, also a few stately elms on each side of Kennerley's Lane, which made that part one of the most lonely spots in the district, quite a suitable haunt of Ghosts, Goblins, Tuggins, and Things-i'th'-Edges, with the old Hall for headquarters. . . . But even the rustling of the leaves on the top of the trees filled us all with terror, so much so that we used to run for our lives and dared not look behind us until, out of breath, we reached the top of Church Street, as we never felt safe from those invisible beings until we had reached that point, as there were no houses at that time in Hawthorn Lane'.

In 1843 the school was acquired by Thomas Somerville, a thirty-six years old Scottish schoolmaster. Living in the house beside Somerville in 1851 were his wife, five daughters, two sons, a cook, a housemaid, a nursemaid, a French teacher, and twenty-four boy boarders between the ages of seven and eighteen who came mainly from Lancashire and Cheshire, but included one from Greece and one from Spain. The Hall must still have had considerable land attached to it because Somerville, as well as being a schoolmaster, was described as a farmer of 140 acres with ten labourers. The house was certainly much bigger than it is now: the 1872 25″ O.S. plan shows a considerable L-shaped addition. Part of this addition is shown in the illustration: a large, bleak, two-storey annexe jutting westwards from the north end of the house—no doubt providing extra accommodation for the school.

Advertising his school in 1874, Somerville described it as a 'classical, commercial, and mathematical academy. . . . The mode of teaching pursued by Dr. Somerville and qualified Assistants equally avoids the drudgery of the *old* system, and the superficiality of the *new*. The utmost care is taken that the Pupil should thoroughly understand the reasons of everything as he proceeds, and that nothing be passed over in a careless or indifferent manner. No corporal punishment whatever is used, but to secure the order and regularity requisite in a school, recourse is had to a sort of school currency, the representative of labour cheerfully performed.—Fines in the

48. Hawthorn Hall School, before 1898

peculiar currency are levied in proportion to the faults committed, and, by such means, the encouragement and punishment of Pupils promote their intellectual and moral education'.

Somerville (whose son became medical officer of Wilmslow) died in 1883, and the school was taken over by J. McKim. But in 1896 the building had been 'untenanted for several years', was 'prominently before the public', and seemed likely to be soon demolished: Miss Eliza Bower had recently died and the Hall, by order of Chancery, was sold to 'the present various owners'. The illustration shown here has been dated 'before 1898', and it seems likely that the addition to the Hall was removed about this time because Andrew Pearson, writing in 1897, said the house 'has been recently renovated. This has produced a marked change in the appearance of the old structure'. The 1898 25″ O.S. plan shows the building reduced to its present-day size.

The Quaker Meeting-house

Although Cheshire did not feel the first shock of George Fox's electrifying message when it flashed through the northern counties during the great foundation years of Quakerism, 1652–1653, the sense that the county came rather late into the picture is really an illusion, the effect of enormous evangelistic activity packed into a few months. It was, in fact, no later than October 1653 that the Quaker missionaries John Lawson and Richard Hubberthorne arrived in Wrexham and shortly afterwards in Chester. In November Hubberthorne was thrown into Chester gaol; there he met and convinced the puritan preacher Thomas Yarwood who presently carried the new teaching to a group of Seekers at Mobberley.

The Seekers, a separatist sect who anticipated the Quakers, frequently merged with them under the charismatic influence of Fox and the Quaker publishers of truth. Little is known about the group at Mobberley: we are simply told it was their custom 'when met together, neither to preach nor pray vocally, but to read the scriptures and discourse of religion, expecting a further manifestation'. The early association of Quakers with Mobberley is still witnessed by the small, neatly-walled square of their burial ground near the edge of Lindow Moss; and on the first page of

49. Quaker Meeting-house, Altrincham Road

the first volume of the sufferings of Cheshire Quakers is an account of the arrival of troopers on 3 July 1665 at a meeting for worship in the house of Edward Alcocke of Mobberley. The eighteen worshippers were arrested, imprisoned for two months, released, then rearrested several times during the same year. Friends who visited them in gaol were arrested for good measure, and the only food they had was passed to them through the prison windows.

Although the earliest Quaker meetings in the area were thus held in private houses in Mobberley, the first meeting-house was the building illustrated here, on the

Altrincham Road in the township of Morley in Wilmslow. Morley Monthly Meeting for the Quakers of east Cheshire was established in 1668; and Quakers from Wilmslow and neighbourhood continued to meet in the Morley meeting-house until the present one, much nearer the centre of Wilmslow, was built on Stamford land in 1831.

V · Savour of the past, taste of the future

The good old days

Stephen Beswick, known as Jarmug because he always drank out of a jam jar, lived with his mother in the last house on the right in Newtown (now Park Road). He was her only son and he never married. When she died he took to living in a large bacon box just beyond the wire netting of the henpen in the garden of 55 Manchester Road. He made a living by delivering coal in a two-wheeled cart.

'From the stories of the pranks played upon him the Wilmslow hermit must have been the oddest of men. . . . At the time of the death of the late Rev. Emery Bates, some of the young fellows in the village told Jarmug he was to be the next rector . . . one Sunday morning he marched behind a band, dressed in a frock coat and tall hat, from Fulshaw Cross to the church'.

'At four o'clock in the morning [of Saturday, 8 May 1909] Inspector Dean and a constable made a raid on the rude shelter occupied for the last two and a half years by Stephen Beswick, at Hill Top, Wilmslow. The officers found him asleep, but on being aroused he went quietly with the officers to the police station. After appearing before a magistrate he was taken to Bucklow Union Workhouse'. 'The poor chap developed a cancer of the lip and that's why he was taken'.

'Jarmug used to walk [with] a strange, bobbing gait, reminiscent of the way music hall artists used to make their entrance in Victorian days. . . . He used to walk through the village singing to himself, pomp-adomp-apomp, just like that. . . . He was a rare'un, was Jarmug'.

Girls beneath the Edge

Girls in boaters cycle serenely along empty lanes beneath the bosky hill; the only other movement is cottage smoke flowing gently into the summer air. Where the girls are cycling is the Hough, the old township which, at its northern tip, includes the village of Wilmslow itself, but which gets its Anglo-Saxon name from the way, in the south, the land rises to meet the Edge.

By this time Alderley Edge had long been popular—with the 'cottontots', 'invited hither by the fine air, and the extensive and interesting views of the surrounding country', and with the trippers from Manchester. But the Hough, in Earwaker's

50. Stephen Beswick, c.1908

51. Girls cycling near Alderley Edge

opinion, contained 'very little of any interest'; yet it preserves today the largest number of ancient farms of any township in Wilmslow—snugly strung on a pendant of snaking lanes.

At the end of June 1876 the Alderley Edge Bicycle Club was formed. By December 2 it had made fifteen active members, and was 'getting on as well as can be expected'. Indigo blue was decided on as the club colour, and members were to wear a small skull cap with the initials A.E.A.B.C. embroidered on the front.

The Post Office

Dapper as gendarmes, and sporting a rich variety of moustaches, Wilmslow's Edwardian postal staff pose behind their premises at the top of Church Street. The first regular postmaster in Wilmslow was Dr. Joseph Dean, appointed about 1840. Before then the few letters brought to the area by coach were left at the inn where the horses were changed, and 'found their way to their destination with more or less expedition, usually the latter'. Even under Dean (who, rather surprisingly, was also surgeon and country practitioner) there was no organized delivery, but 'the ten letters *per diem*, which literally passed through his hands, enjoyed a reasonable chance of ultimate delivery, for sooner or later the capacious pocket which contained a case of lancets in contact with a thin bundle of letters would appear at every corner of the parish'. With the introduction of the penny post and the opening of the railway, business picked up, and Dean's eight sons and two daughters 'enabled him to cope successfully with the delivery of letters to the various parts of the district'.

Wilmslow's first post office was in Dean's house on the east side of Grove Street. About 1850 he was succeeded by James Taylor who in 1864 built a new post office on part of Dean's garden. As well as being postmaster Taylor trebled up as schoolmaster and parish clerk; for good measure he boarded the curate. Like Dean he had a sizeable family—five daughters and two sons. But now there was a regular letter carrier: Benjamin Kelsall, former handloom weaver. 'The simple ways of a bygone age seemed to cling to honest Benjamin, and a greater contrast rarely presents itself than was manifested between him and the sprightly, trim, half-military-looking letter-carriers who now so briskly traverse the district. The official costume was donned of late years, but it never lent itself pleasantly to his civilian figure and his loose and easy gait. Our village postman moved along, finding in every cottager a friend, for whom he had a kindly word and a ready smile, and in every dog he found a foe for whom his stout staff was ever held in readiness. He loved his occupation, and dispensed his letters as personal favours, and it may have been that he regarded with pardonable self-complacency the development of the postal business which throve under his distribution, pretty much as a gardener takes the chief credit for the vegetables and flowers which spring around him in his garden'.

Under Taylor more systematic delivery was undertaken, and in 1854 Alderley Edge got its own sub-post office and its own letter carrier. For delivery in the outlying Wilmslow areas there was one boy, William Bracegirdle, 'whose active life in the open air has laid a foundation of robust health' which stood him in good stead in his later occupation of local board road mender. 'Bracegirdle's morning round beyond the village commenced at Fulshaw, thence to Morley, and after partaking of the dinner for which he had acquired a splendid appetite, he proceeded to Stannilands, thence to Finney Green, Dean Row, and, if needful, to Newton Hall. One distribution only was made daily. The limits for free delivery were narrow, and did not extend much beyond the village. A penny a mile was charged for delivery beyond the limit'.

In the last week of October 1850 a daily average of 96 letters were delivered from the Wilmslow office: 57 to Wilmslow, 34 to Chorley (Alderley Edge), and 5 to Monksheath. In 1885 the daily figures for the same area had increased twenty-fold to a total of 1,955: Wilmslow (by five carriers) 800, Alderley Edge (by four carriers) 1,000, Styal ('formerly supplied by Messrs Greg's bag from Wilmslow') 100, Monksheath 55.

Taylor (who by 1861 had added shopkeeper to his occupations) died in 1868. His widow, Eliza, succeeded him and acted as postmistress and ironmonger until 1873, when she was succeeded by her daughter, Maria. In 1884 the post office moved across Grove Street to accommodation in the handsome new block of six shops built on the site of the Grove's bowling green. The 1898 25″ O.S. plan shows it still there, but by 1909 it had moved to the top of Church Street, next to the bank on the corner, and it was at the rear of this building that the photograph was taken.

The date of the photograph must be some time after 1901 because Miss Taylor's place was taken on 1 October 1901 by Mr. W.S. Cobb, and the postmaster in the photograph (second from the right on the front row) is Mr. Harry Potts. Everyone else's name, too, is known: from left to right, back row, Sam Adshead, Thomas

52. Post Office staff, shortly after 1900

Bradbury (who was postman for forty-two years in the Morley ward area), Walter Henshaw, George Mottershead, —— Jones, Harold Perceval; middle row, Lionel Traill, Sam Burgess, Sydney Wood, Alfred Burgess, Joe Bower, Tom Ainsworth, Bill Percival, Billy Bowers; front row, Katie Hough, Ellen Dix, Fred Wood, Harry Potts, Helena Hough.

The Town Band

Today, bandstands are being demolished, and the regular, manly blare of public, home-made music has largely departed from the towns. In Wilmslow St. Bartholomew's band and school bands are alive and well, and at Christmas time the Salvation Army is loyal to old traditions; but the big and frequent occasions for brass and silver bands—church processions, friendly societies' walks, the carnival ('the best in Cheshire')—are almost gone.

In the first half of the nineteenth century ensembles were modest. For Water Lane Wesleyan Sunday School the 'great day of the year' was an annual walk through the main streets of the old village: the scholars came to a halt on the open space at the top of Church Street and sang, to the accompaniment of John Bradley, clarionet, James Dooley, 'cello, Job Arden, double bass, and William Alcock, serpent.

In his youth Andrew Pearson and six or seven of his friends used to meet in the old Gas House in Church Street 'for mutual improvement in music, grammar, and other branches'; as an Amateur String Band they also met weekly in the Water Lane school room, 'but we had to buy our own candles'. Some of the violins used by the members were made by Job Arden, 'hardware, glass, etc. dealer' of Grove Street: he made over five hundred instruments, 'the quality of which will entitle him to rank among the noted violin makers of the Nineteenth Century'.

By the end of the nineteenth century the really big occasion required orchestration of Berlioz proportions. On 22 June 1897 five or six thousand men, women, and children assembled on Lindow Common to celebrate the Queen's diamond jubilee, and to receive forty-eight acres of racecourse as a gift from alderman John Royle. The day was a general holiday, the village was artistically decorated, Queen's weather

53. Anticipation: St. Bartholomew's band outside a public house in Denton

54. Preparation: assembling on the fair-ground for the Friendly Societies' walk

55. Jubilation: marching up Grove Street in celebration of Queen Victoria's diamond jubilee, 22 June 1897

prevailed. Members and officials of the urban district council, friendly societies, the police, the fire brigade, and all the schools, headed by three brass bands, marched in procession to the Common where they sang verses to the Queen specially composed by Andrew Pearson. After the ceremony the procession reformed, marched again through the village, had tea, and finished with fireworks and a large bonfire on the rectory fields.

The Fire Brigade

Wilmslow fire station was originally in Green Lane. About 1898 the firemen were: Harry Bailey, driver, Chris Bilsborough, Jabez Birtles, Fred Bushill, ——— Challis, Herbert Henshaw, Jack Howard, Charlie Hoyland, Bill Mottram, Jack Mottram, William Mottram, and Andrew Price. In 1909 the brigade moved to premises in Hawthorn Street which were purpose-built but still managed to accommodate the parish library. In 1912 the station was connected to the telephone system.

Until 1924 the fire engine was drawn by cab horses. When the hooter sounded from the top of the gas holder horses were unhitched from cabs wherever they were, ridden madly to the station, hitched to the engine, and raced to the fire; 'delay, of course, was inevitable and was appreciated by every small boy in the district who arrived at the fire long before the brigade'. On 29 July 1924, however, Superintendent Beckwith of Stockport Fire Brigade introduced Wilmslow firemen to a new solid-tyred motor fire engine, and they had their first run out in it. The chief fire officer was Harry Parker (formerly of the Manchester Fire Brigade), the driver was Sgt. A. Bradbury, and the firemen were A. Acton, H. Antrobus, T. Bennett, S. Garner, W. Greenhall, H. Higginson, F. Mottram, R. Owen, J. Percival, and F. Whittle.

In the early 1920s serious fires in Wilmslow cost about £30 to put out. On 7 December 1921 the old Public Hall in Swan Street burnt down. Ten firemen, working between thirteen and twenty hours apiece, were paid a total of £28 17 0; twenty-three helpers, paid mainly four shillings each, got £5 8 6; the horses cost a guinea, and so did the use of the engine; Mr. J.R. Mottram's ladders cost a pound: total £35 5 6. On Thursday, 4 October 1923, the Carrs Mill burnt down. The call came

56. Horse-drawn fire engine behind Fulshaw Hall, c.1898

57. Motor-driven fire engine, c.29 July 1924

at 6.32 p.m. The brigade left the engine house at 6.40 p.m., and arrived at the fire at 6.53 p.m. Nine firemen worked between eight and twenty hours each and were paid £21; twenty-three helpers and pumpers, working from three to seven hours and receiving six shillings each, were paid £2 8 0; horses and engine again cost two guineas, and the 'cleaning appliance' £1 4 0; A. Antrobus was paid one shilling and four pence for oil, the gasmen two shillings for the alarm, and refreshments cost £1 2 6; total £33 16 0.

The fire brigade is still manned partly by 'retained' firemen, though they are more difficult to come by now. They give eighteen hours cover, for which they are paid a retaining fee of £93 per annum during the first three years, and £116 subsequently. Their function is to man the second machine which leaves within five minutes of the first. For a 'turn-out' they are paid £1.75 for the first hour, and 78p per hour afterwards. For an 'attendance' (that is, if they arrive within five minutes and the second machine has left with a full crew) they receive 95p. Today there is no public hooter or siren, but personal summons of each fireman through his own portable 'bleeper', wired in to the teleprinter alarm alerted from Chester.

The present fire station in Altrincham Road is the headquarters of B District of the Cheshire County Fire Brigade. It cost £54,000 and was opened on 5 June 1964. There are two Rolls-Royce-powered Dennis 'water-tender-ladders', each carrying four hundred gallons of water and a forty-five foot aluminium extension ladder. In the twelve months ending 30 December 1972 the brigade responded to 545 calls.

Death of the horse

Pony and trap and party pause before setting out for market from a smallholding on Lindow Moss; in the corner are rhubarb, two handsome cabbages, and a barrow-load of peat. In 1969 Mr. Warburton remembered how, before the first world war, outlying farm people used to come into Wilmslow in their traps and leave them behind his father's shop while they did their shopping.

Horses endured for a long time. It had been expected that the railways would kill them. Writing in 1897 Pearson tells the story of 'old Jenny Barker, who lived on

58. Pony and trap on Lindow Moss

Parsonage Green, and [was] well known some fifty years ago'. She kept a horse and cart and carried parcels to and from Stockport twice a week; she also transported household coal from Poynton. A few weeks before the railway was due to open, in May 1842, somebody asked her what she would do for a living. She said, 'I cannot say, mon. One thing is certain, the old horse will have to be shot, and there will be nothing but the workhouse for me'. But, in fact, nothing of the kind happened: Jenny remained the village carrier till her death; and, says Pearson, 'could the old woman come again and take her stand in modern Wilmslow, she would see more clearly that instead of railways doing away with horses, the opposite has been the result'.

It was the car which killed the horse, but it took a long time to do so: views of Wilmslow before the second world war are pervaded with horses; tractors did not replace horses on farms till after the war; and Bourne's, corn dealers and provision merchants of Grove Street, closed only in 1966. On the other hand, leaving aside tradesmen's horses, perhaps only two private horses were seen about Wilmslow by 1934, one of them the governess cart belonging to the rector.

59. Dr. John Gilmore and family

Birth of the motor

Riding in this Wilmslow car, registered before 1921, is Dr. John Gilmore of Victoria Road. Beside him is his chauffeur, Mr. Arthur Williamson of Hawthorn Street. In the back are Mrs. Gilmore and their eldest son Jack.

The motoring age had dawned on Wilmslow at the beginning of the century. In February 1908 the *Advertiser* was waiting with apprehension for the beginning of 'the dusty season': 'the dust nuisance is bound to come and it will be worse than last year or any previous year, for the simple reason that we shall have more motors on the highways'. That same month the Council was worried about the wear and tear in Dean Row: 'this heavy motor traffic has become a serious question in many places; it is one of those things which require careful watching. Great damage is often done to the highways . . . the roads are cut up by these heavy machines'.

About the same time William Firth was fined ten shillings with costs at Macclesfield County Sessions for allowing too much smoke to escape from his car. Constable Chappell said he saw the defendant 'on a light motor car'; he was allowing too much black smoke and vapour to escape, and horses were restive 'on passing the motor'. Chairman: 'You were burning bad coal?'. Defendant: 'I was just using coal on account of the coke being inferior'.

The old community

Through a gentle haze bygone Wilmslow raises its assorted roofs undemonstratively to the sky. The countryside—tree-lined river, haystack, chopped wood—reaches right to the old heart: the church, the cornmill, the site of Bollin Hall.

In the seventeenth century Wilmslow was almost entirely agricultural: there were few shopkeepers and independent craftsmen, but numerous yeomen, husbandmen, and poor people dependent on common, waste, and smallholding. In the eighteenth century domestic industry flourished, but it was still a sideline, combined with husbandry. Then came factories and increased industrialisation: in 1851, out of a total employed population of 2,494, over 400 worked at home on cotton and silk handlooms, and nearly 500 were employed in textile factories. Yet even so, there were still 132 farms in Wilmslow, and a quarter (in Fulshaw a third) of the employed population were agricultural workers and farmers.

By the mid-nineteenth century changes were beginning which heralded the Wilmslow of today. In 1842 the railway came, bringing middle class commuters from Manchester; in 1857 Lord Stamford sold his half of Wilmslow, and the biggest buyer took down William Bower's factory in Church Street because he wanted to see Wilmslow a residential district.

Since then Wilmslow has warded off industry, but welcomed the commuter. Sometimes slowly, sometimes swiftly, Wilmslow is losing the obvious evidences of its

60. Wilmslow from the north-east

past: venerable farms are built over, ancient roads widened, old houses demolished. Increasingly, we become dependent on old documents, old illustrations, old reminiscences, and seeing eyes, to recapture the Wilmslow of yesterday, to savour a world 'as old as man himself . . . a world dependent upon human muscular power, the muscular power of draught animals . . . a hand-made world throughout, a slow world, a world without power, a world in which all things were made one by one'.

Envoi

Home-spun poetry and nineteenth century local history were natural bed-fellows. Andrew Pearson used his own and other people's verses liberally, and the sober and statistical Alfred Fryer often quoted poetry in honour of his friends, alive and dead. When local history ceased to be a domestic industry and entered a factory phase its operatives were, perhaps, less inclined to break into song. But now the burgeoning of local history societies promises the renewal of a folk craft, and in this spirit the following poems have been spun by a thirteen years-old piecer.

Wilmslow Poems

by Paul Hodson

St. Bartholomew's

Stones climb to a lofty tower,
Heavy time-troubled gate stands forlorn.
Mildewed memories moulder in the graveyard.
Time ticks on the high clock.

When a church was a church
People
Praised the Lord
Amen.

But now
Oblivion
For religion
Means the end.

Swift-seizing shoppers
Never think
Of old St. Barts.

But
In the church
Life flourishes,
Regardless of belief.

The George and Dragon

The pub makes the place—
So the locals say—
Especially so with the George and Dragon.

Once—
Years ago, in unknown antiquity, so it seems—
Wilmslow was *here*.

Essential pump, providing water,
Under a pyramid roof;
Just like the cottages, living life,
Under their patient thatch.
The George and Dragon,
Relief after tiring days;
And, guarding all, the church,
Looking after problems
And God.

One by one they disappeared
Before an increasing standard of living.
Only pub and church
Function still.
Which one is doing better?

The Bollin

Down to the Carrs
By the bumpy bridle path
Where the Bollin winds its way.

In the sand-suspended water
Lie tiny stones,
Water-caressed through time.

Undistinguished bricks in the bank
Bastion a bridge
Built by lordly generosity
For the sum of sixty pounds.

The Bollin's done many things:
Divided demesnes, driven mills,
Drowned children in recent times.
But still it meanders on
Unchanged by the centuries.

Quarry Bank Mill

Industry comes to rural Wilmslow
Bringing its train of riches
And crowded poverty.

Quarry Bank Mill—
Samuel Greg, a man to make millions:
'Who wants cottage spinning,
Scattered round the countryside?
Concentrate!
And immediately improve'.

Water power's heyday—
Additions,
Improvements.
Give them tiny cottages, but give them a church.

Gradual decreasing.
'Why? We've still got water
Cheap and accessible
And labour too'.
But inevitable decline.

Today, once more rural,
A quaint old relic
Of how twentieth century Wilmslow
Began.

Rise and Fall

'Come and live in Wilmslow,
We'll pay your train fares',
Said the machine-moneyed millionaires.
Medieval Wilmslow turns abruptly to a tall town.

Lines to Styal and Stockport,
Altrincham and Crewe,
Red-brick bridges to carry the crowds.

Steam supreme!

The all-effacing motor car arrives;
Decline in demand;
Centre shifting outwards;
Steam surpassed;
The Railway rules no more.

Grove Street

Bank Square to Barclays:
Quarter mile of concentrated chaos.
Crowded crushing,
Housewives' hubbub,
Randomly rushing
For food.

They say they are hurrying,
Hustling,
Bustling,
But 'Fancy seeing you here'
Takes half a hurried hour.

In Wilmslow's centre
For a century
Business is better than ever before.

Ice!

A walk—why not?
Car-caressed feet need
A change.

Off for the Common;
Frost still bites deep,
Children chatter,
Warmth-wrested, cold.

Cross the road quickly:
Hated cars clash
With natural nature.

The Black Lake shimmers
Expectant,
Ready for freezing feet.

Ice!
Children clamour for consent:
'No, it's too thin'
'We don't care'
'No!'

Race you round.
Disappointment forgotten,
Trees climbed,
Stones thrown,
Skittering over the ice,
Home for tea.

Children

Bricks and white windows,
Seagull-soaked field,
Grey tarmac playground,
Children!
Pouring out to play.

Big ones and little ones,
Quiet ones and boyish ones,
Sweet little brown ones with curly hair.

Chancel Lane collapsing,
Where to site a new school?
At green Gorsey Bank.

Here was once a workhouse,
Poor little poor boys,
Now happy little rich boys
Have taken their place.

Back of School

Cinders irritate my feet,
Bare banks curve to corridoring chestnuts,
Break-out to the back of school!

Nettles waylay me—
Yearly razed, yearly returning:
Tumultuous tussocks
Like the hair of the children they trip.

Dusky intersection:
Ancient lamp-post guards
A trampled triangular garden.

Broad, quiet, peaceful,
Boards on both sides.
Stillness suddenly shattered
By busy Broad Walk.

A Day Out

Wilmslow Historical Society
At its early morning meeting place
Shivers in the spiteful summer rain.

Lack of coach creates confusion,
Its arrival even more.
But our Chairman organises
And we're off.

Sleepy legs stretch below the stately house,
Where H***** H***** cruises quite at home
Discussing differences of style.

On to angular Industrial Archaeology.
Here too the Chairman leads us on
Past huge tap-hammers and
begrimed blast furnaces,
Under the shadow of a mysterious warehouse.

Returning home when dusk dulls vision,
'It wasn't so bad
After all'.

Going Home

Light-littered station,
Black banks frowning
On shining shops
Smiling success.

Victorian residences
Dishevelled but desirable
Lead to green suburbs,
Happiness infectious,
Home!

Sources and Abbreviations

Bagshaw: Samuel Bagshaw, *History, gazetteer & directory of the county . . . of Chester*, 1850.

Buxton: E.J.M. Buxton, *A guide to the parish church of St. Bartholomew, Wilmslow*, 1936 (reprinted 1938).

Census: Public Record Office, census enumerators' schedules of returns, Wilmslow: 1841, H.O. 107/115; 1851, H.O. 107/2161, 2162.

C.R.O.: Cheshire Record Office.

Dodgson: J.McN. Dodgson, *The place-names of Cheshire*, part I, vol. XLIV, English Place-Name Society, 1970.

Earwaker: J.P. Earwaker, *East Cheshire: past and present*, vol. 1, 1877; vol. 2, 1880.

Everitt: Alan Everitt, 'Farm labourers', *The agrarian history of England and Wales*, IV, 1500–1640, 1967.

Fryer: Alfred Fryer, *Wilmslow graves and grave thoughts from Wilmslow*, 1886.

Historical collector: The Cheshire and Lancashire historical collector, edited by T. Worthington Barlow, vol. I, 1853.

Lancaster: Ruth Lancaster, 'Quarry Bank Mill, Styal, 1784–1850', thesis submitted for a teaching certificate at Derby Training College, May 1959.

L.R.O.: Lancashire Record Office.

Murray: Robert Murray, 'Quarry Bank Mill: 1. The story of the mill. 2. The medical service', *British journal of industrial medicine*, vol. 15, 293–298, 1958; vol. 16, 61–67, 1959.

Nicholson: J. Holme Nicholson, 'Wilmslow church and its monuments', *Transactions of the Lancashire and Cheshire Antiquarian Society*, vol. VIII, 1890, 53–62.

Norbury: William Norbury, 'Chorley Hall, and other buildings in its neighbourhood', *Transactions of the Lancashire and Cheshire Antiquarian Society*, vol. IV, 1886, 98–114.

Ormerod: George Ormerod, *The history of the county palatine and city of Chester*, second edition revised by Thomas Helsby, three vols., 1882.

Pearson: Andrew Pearson, *Wilmslow: past and present*, second edition, 1901.

Potter: Simeon Potter, 'Cheshire place-names', *Transactions of the Historic Society of Lancashire and Cheshire*, vol. 106, 1955, 1–22.

W.A.: Wilmslow advertiser.

Wilmslow Trust: The Wilmslow Trust, *Buildings of architectural and historical interest in Wilmslow & Alderley Edge*, [1970].

Notes to the text

Each of the following notes is introduced by catchwords extracted from the text on the page indicated. Full titles of books referred to here in abbreviated form will be found in the preceding *Sources and abbreviations.*

INTRODUCTION

5 There is a story told by Evelyn Waugh: Osbert Sitwell, *Laughter in the next room*, 1949, 349, quoted by H.P.R. Finberg, *Local history: objective and pursuit*, 1967, 19.

5 Earwaker, devoting one page . . . to the industrial village of Bollington: Earwaker, II, 333.

5 To neighbouring Pott Shrigley: Earwaker, II, 315–332.

5 10,700 recorded burials: F.S. Stancliffe, *Wilmslow parish magazine*, February 1960.

6 'Paul saw drops of sweat . . .': D.H. Lawrence, *Sons and lovers*, Penguin Books, 1967, 173.

6 he quotes from Eric Gill: W.G. Hoskins, *Local history in England*, 1959, 25.

7 Andrew Pearson . . . had no doubts: Pearson, 67.

7 Hoskins has calculated: W.G. Hoskins, 'Provincial towns in the early sixteenth century', *Transactions of the Royal Historical Society*, fifth series, vol. 6, 1956, 18.

8 Professor Everitt reckons: Everitt, 398–9.

8 not all 'unrelieved hardship and monotony': Everitt, 430.

8 In a sample of about three hundred labourers' probate inventories: Everitt, 431–2.

8 a 'commercial nexus between masters and men': Everitt, 440.

8 'farmworkers were ceasing to be thought of as respected members': Everitt, 442.

8–9 'the poor people are all vile Rogues & thieves': Martha Finney to Samuel Finney, 15 June 1766, C.R.O. DFF/28/8.

9 In 1851: these and subsequent details for 1851 are from the census, 1851.

9 Today these streets have a population of . . .: these and subsequent contemporary figures are based on the 1973 *Register of electors*.

11 the Carrs, by their name and their feel: Old Norse *kjarr* brushwood, marsh (Dodgson, 231), meadow recovered from bog (*Shorter Oxford English dictionary*).

12 The director of a regional civic trust: *The Guardian*, 19 March 1973.

12 An architect sees some local preservationists: *W.A.*, 8 March 1973.

13 The chairman of a preservationist society: *The Guardian*, 19 March 1973.

13 Dukenfield Hall . . . a cruck house sheathed in Jacobean brick: pointed out by Mr. S. Wheeler and Dr. R.W. Brunskill.

13 'surely our district's nearest approach to squalor': *W.A.*, 25 January 1973.

13 schemes 'carried out with the aid of repair and improvement grants': *Country life*, September 14/21 1972, 623.

I The Beginnings

William's Hill

27 'William's mound': for Wilmslow's place-names see Dodgson, Potter. Wilmslow, 'Wighelm's mound' (Dodgson, 220), 'Wilhelmes hlaw [burial mound]' (Potter, 10).

27 the name is confined to the church and churchyard: Earwaker, I, 42.

27 the charters recording these transactions: Earwaker, I, 42–4.

A Seven hundred years-old stream

28 'Let all men, present and to come': L.R.O. DDTr 19.

28 in discussing this charter Earwaker says: Earwaker, I, 43.

28 then branches off northwards: in *The story of Wilmslow*, 1971, 8, I described the rest of the stream as running past Oversleyford brickworks, and so continuing to coincide with the parish and urban district boundaries. However, although the 1954 6″ O.S. map does indicate a stream by the brickworks, there is no evidence of it in Greenwood or Swire and Hutchings, and it would, in any case, exclude Ullerswood (Dodgson, 230).

Bollin Hall

33 Andrew Pearson, writing in 1897: Pearson, 31.

33 Earwaker, too, had it described to him: Earwaker, I, 61.

33 William Norbury, on the other hand: Norbury, 101. Ormerod, who collected his material between 1813 and 1819, said Bollin Hall 'is an ancient brick-built farm-house, situated east of the Bollin, and probably occupies the site of the original seat of the Fittons', Ormerod, III, 591.

II The Centre

Church and Village

35 a description . . . of all these clustering cottages: Fryer, 58–60.

35 By 1851: census, 1851.

St. Bartholomew's

36 the base of the tower may be fifteenth century: Wilmslow Trust, 2.

36 Fryer points: Fryer, 61.

37 faculties obtained in 1862 and 1897: Wilmslow parish records, schedule 5, Additions, alterations, restorations.

37 the great extension of the churchyard in 1862: Plan of land in Wilmslow, 8 January 1862, C.R.O. DDT.

37 'disastrous restoration': Buxton, 19.

37 'the flooring of the pews generally was so rotten': Fryer, 63.

37 faculty of 17 July 1862: Wilmslow parish records, schedule 5.

37 'wanton destruction': Buxton, 7.

37 Before the Reformation there were few pews: *Historical collector*, no. 1, April 1853, 7.

37 'the effect of looking down from the galleries': Fryer, 63.

38 'wretched gross Daubing of Moses and Aaron': *Historical collector*, no. 1, April 1853, 8.

38 'grotesque decorations': Fryer, 64.

38 'a lofty, modern chancel arch': Nicholson, 57.

38 'beautified' with carving: Buxton, 18.

38 faculty of 28 October 1897: Wilmslow parish records, schedule 5.

38 'mutilation' of the screens: Buxton, 17.

38 'there are now only a few scraps of the old wood left': Buxton, 18.

38 'the indignity of a rood loft': Buxton, 7.

38 'the simple and dignified brestsummer board': Buxton, 18.

The Old Rectory?

38 a siege during the civil war: Earwaker, I, 91.

40 strong local tradition: Earwaker, I, 89–90; Pearson, 13.

40 probate inventory of Thomas Wright, 1661: C.R.O. WS.

40 terrier of the rectory, 1663: C.R.O. EDV 8/91/1.
40 as he reported to his bishop: Articles of enquiry, 1778, C.R.O. EDV 7/1/110.
41 the house of Henry Trafford: probate inventory, 1591, C.R.O. WS.
41 Earwaker evidently thought so: Earwaker, I, 90.

AN ARRAY OF BOWERS

42 Wills of Ralph (1763), Sarah (1766), and Ralph (1801) Bower: C.R.O. WS.
42 Ralph Bower . . . was a farmer: Norbury, 108–9.
42–3 Fryer says . . . Fryer's description of the churchyard: Fryer, 59.
43 Samuel Finney, however, puts it: *Historical collector*, no. 2, May 1853, 8.

WILLIAM BOWER, 1801–1862

44 Wills of Charles (1806), William (1827), Ralph (1834), and John (1853) Bower: C.R.O. WS.
44–5 He lived . . . at the corner of Manchester Road: census, 1851.
46 Bagshaw's *Cheshire directory* of 1850: Bagshaw, 339.
46 According to Andrew Pearson: Pearson, 52.
46 built a gas works: Pearson, 21.

THE ENDURING TRIANGLE

46 in 1663: glebe terrier, 1663, C.R.O. EDV 8/91/1.
47 by Pearson's time: Pearson, 56.
48 several mills in the Church Street area: Norbury, 109–10; Daniel Lysons, *Magna Britannia*, vol. 2, 1810, 819–21.
48 By 1850: Bagshaw, 339.
48 1901 when the present three houses . . . were built: date-stone.

CORNELIUS SHERRIFFE

48 'all clean and ready': comment by Mr. Arthur Ollerenshaw, 1969.
48 that day he wrote: Wilmslow parish records, schedule 4, Deeds and documents relating to churchyard.

49 'by reason of the great increase of parishioners in the parish of Wilmslow': Sentence of consecration of an additional burying ground, 23 September 1829, Wilmslow parish records, schedule 4.

49 'a worthy couple': Fryer, 59.

50 In 1841: census, 1841.

50 In 1896 . . . In 1900 . . . In 1903: Wilmslow parish records, schedule 4.

THE OLD STREET

50 a fragment of its neighbour up the hill persists: architectural details pointed out by Dr. R.W. Brunskill.

THE STREET OF SHOPS AND PUBS

53 Information supplied by Mr. Arthur Ollerenshaw, 9 December 1969.

THE COMMUNITY STREET

53 'Church Street was a very old-fashioned street then': comment by Mrs. Bradshaw, 2 December 1969.

53 In 1851: census, 1851.

THE TOLL-BAR

55 This originally stood at the end of Brook Lane: *Cheshire notes and queries*, vol. 1, 1896, 14–5.

55 'a band of puppets': *W.A.*, 6 January 1887.

55 The late Mr. Arnold Grimshaw: undated newscutting in Mr. W.R. Hopley's collection.

THE GROVE

57 It was still an inn in 1840: Bollin Fee tithe award and map, C.R.O. EDT.

57 by 1851: census, 1851.

57 as late as 1860: Plan of land at Wilmslow belonging to Sir H. de Trafford, bart., April 21st 1860, C.R.O. DDT.

57 About 1886 a Mr. Mark Wood: Pearson, 55; 'Mr. Mark Wood's plans for alterations to Grove House to be used as shops were referred to Committee', Wilmslow Local Board minutes, 7 January 1887, C.R.O. LUW 1/2.

THE ISLAND

59 By 1841: Bollin Fee tithe award and map, 1840, C.R.O. EDT; census, 1841.

59 In between . . . was a Methodist chapel: Bagshaw, 339; Pearson, 65.

59 successor to the temperance public house... in Bank Square: *W.A.*, 20 September 1957.

61 who reputedly frequently walked to Manchester and back: Pearson, 23.

61 Francis Poole, grocer: Pearson, 21.

THE BLACKSMITH

61 In 1851: census, 1851.

61 ten years earlier: census, 1841.

61 The smithy in Grove Street was towards the south end: Bollin Fee tithe award and map, 1840, C.R.O. EDT.

61 In 1858 Robert Bourne arrived in Grove Street: Information from Mrs. Bourne, 11 December 1969.

61 in (or about) 1884 he built blocks of shops on both sides: date-stone, 1884, in block on west side; 'new buildings now being erected . . . in Grove Street', Wilmslow Local Board minutes, 2 April 1885, C.R.O. LUW 1/2; block on east side in similar style.

62 By this time the smith was S. Lomas: information from Mrs. A.M. Lomas.

62 He began work on the fourth of August, 1914: information from Mr. George Mottershead.

WILMSLOW'S SHOPS

64 speaking of the 1740s he says: T.S. Ashton, *An economic history of England: the 18th century*, 1966, 215.

64 In 1785, however: *ibid*, 216.

64 In the 1740s . . . By 1785: *ibid*, 215, 216.

64 In 1851: census, 1851.

66 In 1858 Robert Bourne arrived with a handcart: information from Mrs. Bourne.

66 In 1868 Clement Owen came . . . in a 'horse drawn pantechnicon': *Owens centenary wine list, 1868–1968*, 1968, 1.

66 Mr. Warburton . . . had been a grocer: information from Mr. Warburton, 5 December 1968.

THE NEW ROAD

66 In the 1770s Samuel Finney wanted to include Wilmslow: *Historical collector*, no. 9, 1 October 1853, 102–3.

67 'this year', says Finney: *Historical collector*, no. 3, June 1853, 30.

68 on that day, the earl of Stamford leased a plot: lease by Lord Stamford to William Gibbon, 1 August 1792, belonging to Mrs. V. Rahim.

68 as late as 1872: 25″ O.S. plan, 1872.

68 In 1851: census, 1851.

68 described as an artist in 1841: census, 1841.

68 he left, at his death in 1853: will of John Bower, 1853, C.R.O. WS.

THE RAILWAY

69 in 1841 the railway added 543 to Wilmslow's population: [*Census*] *abstract of the answers and returns: enumeration and abstract, 1841*, 1843, 31.

69 'excavators' and their families: census, 1841.

69 the newly formed Urban District Council complained bitterly: Wilmslow Urban District Council minutes, 1894–7, C.R.O. LUW 1/5.

69 Bagshaw's directory: Bagshaw, 342.

THE OLD ROAD

71 *Cheshire notes and queries:* vol. 1, 1896, 74–6.

74 a Trafford estate map of 1771: A map of lands in the townships of Hough and Chorley . . . belonging to John Trafford, esq., C.R.O. DDT.

III THE BOLLIN VALLEY

WILMSLOW'S BRIDGES

75 When Samuel Finney returned from London: *Historical collector*, no. 9, 1 October 1853, 101–3.

WILMSLOW'S WEIR

78 In 1246 Richard Fitton had a mill: Earwaker, I, 44.

78 either the medieval mill was on a different site or . . .: pointed out by Mr. H.W. Johnson.

THE SILK MILL

78 William Norbury confidently identifies it: Norbury, 109.

78 the will of John Bower: C.R.O. WS.

THE LAUNDRY

80 The old silk mill burnt down on 4 October 1923: fire brigade accounts in Mr. W.R. Hopley's collection.

80 'situated in the heart of this pretty country district': undated advertisement in Mr. W.R. Hopley's collection.

POWNALL BRIDGE

82 as late as, certainly, 1831: Bryant's map of Cheshire, 1831.

82 neither . . . appear on a map until 1842: first edition, 1″ O.S. map.

82 Originally there was simply a ford across the river: Disputes over damning up of river Bollin, five letters, 1815–8, Quarry Bank records, Manchester Public Libraries, C5/8/6; Lancaster, 17–8.

82 About half a mile away to the north . . . was Norcliffe Hall: Earwaker, I, 141.

82 Also somewhere nearby was a mill: Earwaker, I, 141.

QUARRY BANK MILL

84 after exploring Lancashire and Derbyshire: Lancaster, 1–2; Murray, vol. 15, 294.

84 Greg leased land from Lord Stamford: Murray, 294.

84 Each day two drays: Lancaster, 7.

84 The mill prospered for forty years: Lancaster, 16–29.

84 closed altogether: *W.A.*, 30 October 1959.

SAMUEL GREG, 1756–1834

86 Samuel Greg's father: Murray, vol. 15, 294.

87 'The house', said John Morley: Lancaster, 6.

87 And Catherine Stanley wrote: Lancaster, 6.

QUARRY BANK MILL: THE WATER POWER

87 the earlier history of the place has a legendary air: Lancaster, 2.

89 as a boathouse: information from the Textile Council.

89 From Pownall ford there was a fourteen foot fall in the river: Lancaster, 2.

89 Greg built a tunnel beneath the woods: Lancaster, 18.

THE 'PRENTICE HOUSE

90 The best first-hand information: Murray, vol. 15, 296–7.

90 The information given . . . by Alfred Fryer: Fryer, 81–2.

SPINNERS, WEAVERS, WHEELWRIGHTS

93 Information from Mr. Samuel Henshall, February 1973.

IV HISTORIC HOUSES

PRESTON COTTAGE

94 originally called Preston Lane: Earwaker, I, 167.

94 the inventory which survives: probate inventory of Edmund Dickens, 1628, C.R.O. WS.

94 The early seventeenth century was a period of extensive rebuilding: W.G. Hoskins, 'The rebuilding of rural England, 1570–1640', *Past and present*, 4, November 1953, 44–59; M.W. Barley, *The English farmhouse and cottage*, 1961.

CHORLEY HALL

96 an early fourteenth century house: Wilmslow Trust, 6.

HANDFORTH HALL

96 Earwaker abruptly interjects: Earwaker, I, 263.

97 Ormerod's contention: Ormerod, III, 645.

97–8 the probate inventory which survives of William Brereton . . . 1610: C.R.O. WS.

98 the similarity of this porch to that at Adlington: *cf. Adlington Hall, Cheshire*, English Life Publications Ltd., n.d.

HAWTHORN HALL

100 the 'foundation' charter of the Wilmslow area: L.R.O. DDTr 19.

100 an inventory was made of his house at Hawthorn: probate inventory of John Latham, 1622, C.R.O. WS.

101 William Webb's description of it about 1621: Earwaker, I, 12.

101 Since the seventeenth century: Earwaker, I, 130–2.

101 in his will: Earwaker, *ibid.*

103 a road variously described: *Cheshire notes and queries*, vol. 1, 1896, 76, 119.

103 As a family they attended the Methodist chapel: *Cheshire notes and queries*, vol. 4, 1899, 25.

HAWTHORN HALL SCHOOL

104 Information about the school in its early days is given in *Cheshire notes and queries*, vol. 4, 1899, 25; about its later days, and about Hawthorn Hall at the end of the nineteenth century, in *Cheshire notes and queries*, vol. 1, 1896, 117, 119, and in Pearson, 37.

104 Andrew Pearson describes: Pearson, 35.

104 In 1851: census, 1851.

105 Advertising his school in 1874: *Morris's Cheshire directory*, 1874, 238.

105 'before 1898': Mr. W.R. Hopley's collection.

THE QUAKER MEETING-HOUSE

106 George Fox's electrifying message: W.C. Braithwaite, *The beginnings of Quakerism*, 1955, 51–129.

106 It was, in fact, no later than October 1653: Braithwaite, *ibid*, 123.

106 'when met together . . .': Braithwaite, *ibid*, 125.

106–7 the first page of the first volume: C.R.O. EFC/6/1.

V SAVOUR OF THE PAST, TASTE OF THE FUTURE

THE GOOD OLD DAYS

109 Information from undated (c.May 1959) newscuttings in Mr. W.R. Hopley's collection.

GIRLS BENEATH THE EDGE

109 'invited hither by the fine air': Bagshaw, 342.

109–11 in Earwaker's opinion: Earwaker, I, 143.

111 Alderley Edge Bicycle Club: *W.A.*, 2 December 1876.

The Post Office

111 The main sources of information about the post office are Fryer, 69–72, and Pearson, 17–8. Facts about the postmasters' families are taken from the 1841, 1851, and 1861 census schedules. The names of the postal staff in the photograph are given in an undated newscutting in Mr. W.R. Hopley's collection.

The Town Band

114 Water Lane Wesleyan Sunday School: Pearson, 64.

114 'for mutual improvement in music': Pearson, 66.

114 On 22 June 1897: Pearson, 69.

The Fire Brigade

116–8 The names of members of the fire brigade in 1898 and 1924, and the accounts for fires at the old Public Hall and the Carrs Mill, are contained in Mr. W.R. Hopley's collection. Information about the present-day brigade was given by A.D.O. Lawton, B District, Cheshire County Fire Brigade.

116 'delay, of course, was inevitable': undated newscutting, c.5 June 1964, in Mr. W.R. Hopley's collection.

Death of the horse

118 'old Jenny Barker': Pearson, 61–2.

Birth of the motor

121 registered before 1921: information from Local Taxation Department, Southport.

121 Dr. John Gilmore: undated newscutting in Mr. W.R. Hopley's collection.

121 'the dust nuisance is bound to come': *W.A.*, 14 February 1908.

121 about the same time William Firth was fined ten shillings: *W.A.*, 24 February 1908.

The old community

121 In 1851: census, 1851.

123 'as old as man himself': Eric Gill, quoted by W.G. Hoskins, *Local history in England*, 1959, 25.

Index

Illustrations are indicated in *italics*